Study Guide and Working Pap

COLLEGE ACCOUNTING
A PRACTICAL APPROACH

Study Guide and Working Papers

COLLEGE ACCOUNTING
A PRACTICAL APPROACH
CHAPTERS 1-15

seventh edition

JEFFREY SLATER

Prentice Hall, Upper Saddle River, NJ 07458

Acquisitions editor: *Diane deCastro*
Project editor: *Richard Bretan*
Formatting: *Omegatype Typography, Inc.*
Printer: *Courier Companies, Inc.*

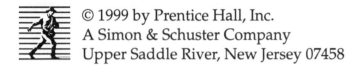

© 1999 by Prentice Hall, Inc.
A Simon & Schuster Company
Upper Saddle River, New Jersey 07458

Printed in the United States of America

10 9 8 7 6 5 4 3 2 1

ISBN 0-13-096154-X

Prentice-Hall International (UK) Limited, *London*
Prentice-Hall of Australia Pty. Limited, *Sydney*
Prentice-Hall Canada Inc., *Toronto*
Prentice-Hall Hispanoamericana, S.A., *Mexico*
Prentice-Hall of India Private Limited, *New Delhi*
Prentice-Hall of Japan, Inc., *Tokyo*
Simon & Schuster Asia Pte. Ltd., *Singapore*
Editora Prentice-Hall do Brasil, Ltda., *Rio de Janeiro*

CONTENTS

INTRODUCTION TO ACCOUNTING CONCEPTS AND PROCEDURES

SELF-REVIEW QUIZ 1-1

PETE O'BRIEN REAL ESTATE

	ASSETS		=	LIABILITIES	+	OWNER'S EQUITY
	Cash	+ Computer Equipment	=	Accounts Payable	+	Pete O'Brien, Capital
TRANSACTION 1						
NEW BALANCE			=			
TRANSACTION 2						
NEW BALANCE			=			
TRANSACTION 3						
ENDING BALANCE		+	=		+	
			=			

SELF-REVIEW QUIZ 1-2

_____

_____

_____

ASSETS						LIABILITIES AND OWNER'S EQUITY					

SELF-REVIEW QUIZ 1-3

B. BING CO.

	ASSETS				=	LIABILITIES	+			OWNER'S EQUITY					
	Cash	+	Accounts Receivable	+	Cleaning Equipment	=	Accounts Payable	+	B. Bing, Capital	-	B. Bing, Withd.	+	Revenue	-	Expenses
Beg. Balance	$10,000	+	$2,500	+	$6,500	=	$1,000	+	$11,800	-	$800	+	$9,000	-	$2,000
1.						=									
Balance						=									
2.						=									
Balance						=									
3.						=									
Balance						=									
4.						=									
Balance		+				=		+		-		+		-	
5															
Ending Balance		+				=		+							

SELF-REVIEW QUIZ 1-4

(1)

_____
_____
_____

(2)

_____
_____
_____

(3)

_____

_____

_____

ASSETS					LIABILITIES AND OWNER'S EQUITY				

FORMS FOR COMPREHENSIVE DEMONSTRATION PROBLEM

(A)

MICHAEL BROWN, ATTORNEY AT LAW

	ASSETS			= LIABILITIES +		OWNER'S EQUITY			
	Cash +	Accounts Receivable +	Office Equipment	= Accounts Payable +	M. Brown, Capital -	M. Brown, Withd.	+ Legal fees -	Expenses
1.								
Balance								
2.								
Balance								
3.								
Balance								
4.								
Balance								
5.								
Balance								
6.								
Balance								
7.								
Balance								
8.								
Balance								
9.								
Ending Balance								

COMPREHENSIVE PROBLEM (CONTINUED)

B (1)

MICHAEL BROWN, ATTORNEY AT LAW
INCOME STATEMENT
FOR MONTH ENDED JUNE 30, 19XX

B (2)

MICHAEL BROWN, ATTORNEY AT LAW
STATEMENT OF OWNER'S EQUITY
FOR MONTH ENDED JUNE 30, 19XX

B (3)

MICHAEL BROWN, ATTORNEY AT LAW
BALANCE SHEET
JUNE 30, 19XX

ASSETS   LIABILITIES AND OWNER'S EQUITY

YOU MAKE THE CALL: CRITICAL THINKING/ETHICAL CASE

CHAPTER 1
FORMS FOR MINI EXERCISES

1. A. Asset
    B. Liability
    C. Owners Equity
    D. Asset
    E. Asset
    F. Asset

2. A. Shift in Assets
    B. Liabilities
    C. Cash

3. A. increase
    B. Shift

4. ___$10,000___
    ___$2,000___
    ___$8,000___

5. Capital
    Rent Expense
    withdrawal
    Hair salon
    fees earned

6. Accounts Payable
    Legal Fees
    earned

7. A. False
    B. True
    C. True
    D. False

8. A. _____
    B. _____
    C. _____
    D. _____
    E. _____
    F. _____
    G. _____
    H. _____

9. A. _____
    B. _____
    C. _____
    D. _____

Name _Lauren Peterson_ Class _Accounting_ Date _Sept. 6_

FORMS FOR EXERCISES

1-1.

A. $5,000

B. $14,000

C. $6,000

1-2.

ASSETS	=	LIABILITIES	+	OWNER'S EQUITY
A. $60,000	=	$5,000		$60,000
B. −$600	=		+	−$600
C. +$900	=	$900	+	

1-3.

AVON'S CLEANERS
BALANCE SHEET
NOVEMBER 30, 19XX

ASSETS				LIABILITIES AND OWNER'S EQUITY				

EXERCISES (CONTINUED)

1-4.

B. WONG

	ASSETS			=	LIABILITIES	+	OWNER'S EQUITY			
	Cash +	Accounts Receivable +	Computer Equipment	=	Accounts Payable	+	B. Wong, Capital	-	B. Wong, Withd.	+ Revenue - Expenses
A. $60,000	+$60,000						+$60,000			
B.			$7,000+		$7,000-					
C. $200									$200	
D. $14,000									$14,000	
E.		$30,000								$30,000
F. $4,000										$4,000
G. $1,500										$1,500
Ending Balance	$30,000	$30,000	$7,000	=	$7,000		$60,000			$30,000

11

EXERCISES (CONTINUED)

1-5.

(A)

FRENCH REALTY
INCOME STATEMENT
FOR MONTH ENDED JUNE 30, 19XX

(B)

FRENCH REALTY
STATEMENT OF OWNER'S EQUITY
FOR MONTH ENDED JUNE 30, 19XX

(C)

FRENCH REALTY
BALANCE SHEET
JUNE 30, 19XX

ASSETS   LIABILITIES AND OWNER'S EQUITY

END OF CHAPTER PROBLEMS

PROBLEM 1A-1 OR PROBLEM IB-1

KAY'S REALTY

	ASSETS			=	LIABILITIES	+	OWNER'S EQUITY
	Cash	+	Equipment	=	Accounts Payable	=	M. Kay, Capital
TRANSACTION A							
NEW BALANCE							
TRANSACTION B							
NEW BALANCE							
TRANSACTION C							
NEW BALANCE							
TRANSACTION D							
ENDING BALANCE							

PROBLEM 1A-2 OR PROBLEM 1B-2

GREEN'S ADVERTISING SERVICE
BALANCE SHEET
SEPTEMBER 30, 19XX

ASSETS			LIABILITIES AND OWNER'S EQUITY		

PROBLEM 1A-3 OR PROBLEM 1B-3

RICK FOX
TYPING SERVICE

	ASSETS			=	LIABILITIES	+	OWNER'S EQUITY			
	Cash +	Accounts Receivable +	Office Equipment	=	Accounts Payable +	R. Fox, Capital -	R. Fox, Withd. +	Typing Revenue -	Expenses
A.	$10,000					+$10,000			
BALANCE									
B.			$4,000		$4,000				
BALANCE									
C.	-$500							+$500	
BALANCE									
D.		-$2,100						+$2,100	
BALANCE									
E.	-$350								+$350
BALANCE									
F.	-$210								+$210
BALANCE									
G.					-$600				+$600
BALANCE									
H.	-$400						-$400		
ENDING BALANCE									

14

Name _Lauren Peterson_ Class _Accounting_ Date _Sept. 21_

PROBLEM 1A-4 OR PROBLEM 1B-4

(A)

WEST STENCILING SERVICE
INCOME STATEMENT
FOR MONTH ENDED JUNE 30, 19XX

Revenue:				
Stenciling Fees				3000 00
Operating Expenses				
Advertising Expense	110 00			
Repair Expense	25 00			
Travel Expense	250 00			
Supplies Expense	190 00			
Rent Expense	250 00			
Total Operating Expenses			825 00	
Net Income			$2175 00	

(B)

WEST STENCILING SERVICE
STATEMENT OF OWNER'S EQUITY
FOR MONTH ENDED JUNE 30, 19XX

J. West, Capital June 1, 19XX				1200 00
Net income for June	2175 00			
Less withdrawls for June	300 00			
Increase in Capital			1875 00	
J. West, Capital June 1, 19XX			$3075 00	

15

PROBLEM 1A-4 OR PROBLEM 1B-4 (CONCLUDED)

WEST STENCILING SERVICE
BALANCE SHEET
JUNE 30, 19XX

ASSETS				LIABILITIES AND OWNER'S EQUITY			
Cash	2300	00		Liabilities			
Accounts Receivable	400	00		Accounts Payable		310	00
Equipment	685	00					
				Owner's Equity			
				J. West, Capital		3075	00
				Total Liabilities and			
Total Assets	$3385	00		Owners Equity		3385	00

PROBLEM 1A-5 OR PROBLEM 1B-5

TOBEY'S CATERING SERVICE

	ASSETS				= LIABILITIES +	OWNER'S EQUITY			
	Cash	+	Accounts Receivable	+	Equipment	=	Accounts Payable	+	J. Tobey, Capital	-	J. Tobey, Withd.	+	Catering Revenue	-	Expenses
10/25										
BALANCE										
10/27										
BALANCE										
10/28										
BALANCE										
10/29										
BALANCE										
11/1										
BALANCE										
11/5										
BALANCE										
11/8										
BALANCE										
11/10										
BALANCE										
11/15										
BALANCE										
11/17										
BALANCE										
11/20										
BALANCE										
11/25										
BALANCE										
11/28										
BALANCE										
11/30										
END BAL.										

PROBLEM 1A-5 OR PROBLEM 1B-5 (CONTINUED)

(2)

TOBEY'S CATERING SERVICE
BALANCE SHEET
OCTOBER 31, 19XX

ASSETS				LIABILITIES AND OWNER'S EQUITY			

(3)

TOBEY'S CATERING SERVICE
INCOME STATEMENT
FOR MONTH ENDED NOVEMBER 30, 19XX

PROBLEM 1A-5 OR PROBLEM 1B-5 (CONTINUED)

(4)

TOBEY'S CATERING SERVICE
STATEMENT OF OWNER'S EQUITY
FOR MONTH ENDED NOVEMBER 30, 19XX

(5)

TOBEY'S CATERING SERVICE
BALANCE SHEET
NOVEMBER 30, 19XX

ASSETS				LIABILITIES AND OWNER'S EQUITY			

CHAPTER 1
SUMMARY PRACTICE TEST:
INTRODUCTION TO ACCOUNTING CONCEPTS AND PROCEDURES

Part 1 Instructions

Fill in the blank(s) to complete the statement.

1. _____ is the recording function of the accounting process.
2. Assets = _____ + Owner's Equity
3. The owner's current investment or equity in the assets of a business is called _____.
4. A list of assets, liabilities, and owner's equity as of a particular date is reported on a _____ _____
5. _____ create an outward or potential outward flow of assets.
6. Revenue earned on an account creates an asset entitled _____ _____.
7. _____ record personal expenses that are not related to the business. They are a subdivision of owner's equity.
8. The _____ _____ reports how well a business performs for a period of time.
9. The _____ _____ _____ _____ is a report that shows changes in capital.
10. The ending figure for capital from the statement of owner's equity is placed on the _____ _____

Part II Instructions

Answer true or false to the following statements.

1. Business transactions are recorded in monetary terms.
2. Assets less Liabilities equals Owner's Equity.
3. Revenue is an asset.
4. Capital means cash.
5. Bookkeeping is 50 percent of accounting
6. The balance sheet lists assets, revenue, and owner's equity.
7. The balance sheet shows where we are now for a specific period of time.
8. Revenue creates an outward flow of assets.
9. Expenses are a subdivision of owner's equity.
10. Withdrawals is the only subdivision of owner's equity.
11. Withdrawals are listed on the income statement.
12. Revenue is a subdivision of owner's equity.

13. Revenues and withdrawals are listed on the income statement.
14. The income statement helps update the statement of owner's equity, and the statement of owner's equity helps update the balance sheet.
15. Withdrawals are listed on the statement of owner's equity.

Part III Instructions

In column B, record the appropriate code(s) that result from recording the transaction in column A.

1. Increase in assets
2. Decrease in assets
3. Increase in liabilities
4. Decrease in liabilities

5. Increase in capital
6. Increase in revenues
7. Increase in expenses
8. Increase in withdrawals

COLUMN A	COLUMN B
1. EXAMPLE: Jim Murray invested $1,000 in his business.	1,5
2. Bought equipment on account for $100.	
3. Paid salaries of $50	
4. Bought additional equipment for $500 cash.	
5. Paid rent expense of $50.	
6. Received $5,000 in cash from revenue earned.	
7. Paid heat expense of $15.	
8. Earned revenue of $500 that will not be received until next month.	
9. Paid amount owed on equipment previously purchased on account.	
10. Paid for cleaning supplies expense, $15.	
11. Customers paid $10 of amount previously owed.	
12. Bought additional equipment of $1,000, half paid in cash and half charged.	
13. Charge customer $100 for services performed	
14. Jim paid home phone bill from the company's cash.	
15. Advertising expense incurred but not to be paid until next month.	

CHAPTER 1   SOLUTIONS TO SUMMARY PRACTICE TEST

Part I

1. bookkeeping
2. liabilities
3. capital
4. balance sheet

5. expenses
6. Accounts Receivable
7. withdrawals
8. income statement

9. statement of owner's equity
10. balance sheet

Part II

1.	true	**6.**	false	**11.**	false
2.	true	**7.**	false	**12.**	true
3.	false	**8.**	false	**13.**	false
4.	false	**9.**	true	**14.**	true
5.	false	**10.**	false	**15.**	true

Part III

1.	1,5	**6.**	1,6	**11.**	1,2
2.	1,3	**7.**	7,2	**12.**	1,2,3
3.	7,2	**8.**	1,6	**13.**	1,6
4.	1,2	**9.**	4,2	**14.**	8,2
5.	7,2	**10.**	7,2	**15.**	7,3

CHAPTER 1
ACCOUNTING RECALL FORMS

Part I

Part II

1. _____
6. _____

2. _____
7. _____

3. _____
8. _____

4. _____
9. _____

5. _____
10. _____

11. _____

12. _____

13. _____

14. _____

15. _____

Name _Lauren Peterson_   Class _Accounting_   Date _Sept. 17_

CONTINUING PROBLEM FOR CHAPTER 1

ELDORADO COMPUTER CENTER

	ASSETS			=	LIABILITIES	+	OWNER'S EQUITY		
	Cash +	Supplies +	Computer Shop Equipment +	Office Equipment =	Accounts Payable +	Freedman, Capital -	Freedman, Withdrawals +	Revenue -	Expenses
a	$4,500+					$4,500+			
BALANCE	4,500					4,500			
b	1,200-		1,200+						
BALANCE	3,300		1,200			4,500			
c	600-			600+					
BALANCE	2,700		1,200	600		4,500			
d		250+			250+				
BALANCE	2,700	250	1,200	600	250	4,500			
e	400-								400+
BALANCE	2,300	250	1,200	600	250	4,500			400
f	250+							250+	
BALANCE	2,550	250	1,200	600	250	4,500		250	400
g	200+							200+	
BALANCE	2,750	250	1,200	600	250	4,500		450	400
h					85+				85
BALANCE	2,750	250	1,200	600	335	4,500		450	485
i	1,200+							1,200+	
BALANCE	3,950	250	1,200	600	335	4,500		1,650	485
j	100-						100+		
END BAL.	3,850 +	250 +	1,200 +	600 =	335	4,500 -	100 +	1,650 -	485

$5,900 = $5,900

24

ELDORADO COMPUTER CENTER
INCOME STATEMENT
FOR THE MONTH ENDED JULY 31, 19XX

ELDORADO COMPUTER CENTER
STATEMENT OF OWNER'S EQUITY
FOR MONTH ENDED JULY 31, 19XX

ELDORADO COMPUTER CENTER
BALANCE SHEET
JULY 31, 19XX

ASSETS   LIABILITIES AND OWNER'S EQUITY

SOLUTIONS TO ACCOUNTING RECALL

Part I

Part II

1. G	**6.** D	**11.**	False; Part of Owner's Equity
2. F	**7.** C	**12.**	True
3. E	**8.** J	**13.**	False; OE will decrease
4. H	**9.** B	**14.**	False; Balance Sheet
5. A	**10.** I	**15.**	True

DEBITS AND CREDITS: ANALYZING AND RECORDING BUSINESS TRANSACTIONS

2

SELF-REVIEW QUIZ 2-1

1. _____		4. _____	
2. _____		5. _____	
3. _____			

SELF-REVIEW QUIZ 2-2

A.

1. Accounts Affected	2. Category	3. ↑↓	4. Rules	5. T Account Update

B.

1. Accounts Affected	2. Category	3. ↑↓	4. Rules	5. T Account Update

C.	1. Accounts Affected	2. Category	3. ↑↓	4. Rules	5. T Account Update			

D.	1. Accounts Affected	2. Category	3. ↑↓	4. Rules	5. T Account Update			

E.	1. Accounts Affected	2. Category	3. ↑↓	4. Rules	5. T Account Update			

SELF-REVIEW QUIZ 2-3

Cash		111
4,500	300	
2,000	100	
1,000	1,200	
300	1,300	
	2,600	

Accounts Payable		211
300	700	

Salon Fees		411
	3,500	
	1,000	

Accounts Receivable		121
1,000	300	

Pam Jay, Capital		311
	4,000	

Rent Expense		511
1,200		

Salon Equipment		131
700		

Pam Jay, Withdrawals		321
100		

Salon Supplies Exp.		521
1,300		

Salaries Expense		531
2,600		

(1)

(2)

(3)

(4)

FORMS FOR COMPREHENSIVE DEMONSTRATION PROBLEM

(1,2,3)

Advertising Expense 511	Gas Expense 512	Salaries Expense 513	Telephone Expense 514

Accounts Payable 211	Mel Free, Capital 311	Mel Free, Withdrawals 312	Delivery Fees Earned 411

Cash 111	Accounts Receivable 112	Office Equipment 121	Delivery Trucks 122

Name _____ Class _____ Date _____

FORMS FOR COMPREHENSIVE DEMONSTRATION PROBLEM (CONTINUED)

(4)

MEL'S DELIVERY SERVICE
TRIAL BALANCE
JULY 31, 19XX

	Dr.	Cr.

(5A)

MEL'S DELIVERY SERVICE
INCOME STATEMENT
FOR MONTH ENDED JULY 31, 19XX

33

FORMS FOR COMPREHENSIVE DEMONSTRATION PROBLEM (CONTINUED)

(5B)

MEL'S DELIVERY SERVICE
STATEMENT OF OWNER'S EQUITY
FOR MONTH ENDED JULY 31, 19XX

(5C)

MEL'S DELIVERY SERVICE
BALANCE SHEET
JULY 31, 19XX

ASSETS			LIABILITIES AND OWNER'S EQUITY		

YOU MAKE THE CALL: CRITICAL THINKING/ETHICAL CASE

_____

_____

_____

_____

_____

_____

_____

_____

_____

_____

_____

_____

_____

_____

_____

_____

_____

_____

_____

_____

_____

_____

_____

_____

_____

_____

_____

_____

CHAPTER 2
FORMS FOR MINI EXERCISES

1.

Cash	110		R. Rich, Capital	311
4/8 2,000	4/14 2,000			3/7 5,000
4/12 6,000				3/9 3,000
				4/12 6,000

2. A. _____ _____ _____ _____

    B. _____ _____ _____ _____

    C. _____ _____ _____ _____

    D. _____ _____ _____ _____

    E. _____ _____ _____ _____

    F. _____ _____ _____ _____

    G. _____ _____ _____ _____

3.

4. _____
    _____
    _____
    _____
    _____
    _____
    _____
    _____
    _____
    _____

5. A. _____
    B. _____
    C. _____
    D _____
    E. _____
    F. _____
    G. _____
    H _____
    I. _____
    J. _____
    K. _____

FORMS FOR EXERCISES

2-1

_____
_____
_____
_____
_____
_____
_____
_____
_____
_____
_____
_____
_____
_____
_____
_____
_____
_____
_____

2-2

1 Accounts Affected	2. Category	3 ↑ ↓	4 Rules	5 T-Account Update

2-3

Account	Category	↑↓	Financial Report

_____
_____
_____
_____
_____
_____
_____

EXERCISES (CONTINUED)

2-4.

	Dr.	Cr.
A.	8	1
B.		
C.		
D.		
E.		
F.		
G.		
H.		
I.		

2-5.

(1)

HALL'S CLEANERS
INCOME STATEMENT
FOR MONTH ENDED JULY 31, 19XX

(2)

HALL'S CLEANERS
STATEMENT OF OWNER'S EQUITY
FOR MONTH ENDED JULY 31, 19XX

EXERCISES (CONTINUED)

(3)

HALL'S CLEANERS
BALANCE SHEET
JULY 31, 19XX

ASSETS			LIABILITIES AND OWNER'S EQUITY		

END OF CHAPTER PROBLEMS

PROBLEM 2A-1 OR PROBLEM 2B-1

Accounts Affected	Category	Inc. / Dec.	Rules	T-Account Update
Ted Williams Capital	Capital	↑	Cr.	T. Williams Capital	Cash $6,000 $6,000
A. Cash	Asset	↑	Dr.	Office Equip. $3,000	Accts. Payable $3,000
Office Equip.	Asset	↑	Dr.	
B. Accts. Payable	Liability	↓	Cr.	Accounts Payable $600	Expenses $600
Accounts Payable	Liability	↓	Cr.	
C. Rent Expense	Expense	↑	Dr.	Cash $800	Revenue $800
Cash	Asset	↓	Dr.	
D. Revenue	Revenue	↑	Cr.	$500	$500
Accounts Receivable	Asset	↑	Dr.	
E. Revenue	Revenue	↑	Cr.	T. Williams Withdrawal Cash $200 $200
Ted Williams withdrawal	withdrawal	↑	Dr.	
F. Cash	Asset	↓	Cr.	

PROBLEM 2A-2 OR PROBLEM 2B-2

Cash	111
(A) 20,000	50 (D)
(C) 3,000	700 (E)
$23,000	800 (G)
	$1,550 = $21,450

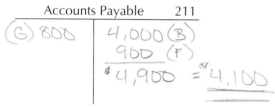

L. White, Withdrawals	312
(D) 50	

Office Equipment	121
(B) 4,000	

Travel Fees Earned	411
	3,000 (C)

Accounts Payable	211
(G) 800	4,000 (B)
	900 (F)
	$4,900 = $4,100

Advertising Expense	511
(E) 700	

L. White, Capital	311
	20,000 (A)

Rent Expense	512
(F) 900	

PROBLEM 2A-3 OR PROBLEM 2B-3

(A)

Cash 111	Accounts Payable 211	Fees Earned 411
(A) 5,000 | 100 (D)	(D) 100 | 1,300 (C)	6,500 (B)
(G) 3,500 | 200 (E)		
8,500 | 400 (F)		
-1,800 | 200 (H)		
New Balance 6,700 | 900 (I)		
1,800		

Accounts Receivable 112	Mike Frank, Capital 311	Rent Expense 511
(B) 6,500 | 3,500 (G)	5,000 (A)	(F) 400

Office Equipment 121	Mike Frank, Withdrawals 312	Utilities Expense 512
(C) 1,300	(I) 900	(E) 200
(H) 200		

(B)

MIKE'S WINDOW WASHING SERVICE
TRIAL BALANCE
MAY 31, 19XX

	Dr.	Cr.
Cash	$6 7 0 0 00	
Accounts Receivable	3 0 0 00	
Office Equipment	1 5 0 0 00	
Accounts Payable		$1 2 0 0 00
Mike Frank, Capital		5 0 0 0 00
Mike Frank, Withdrawal	9 0 0 00	
Fees Earned		6 5 0 0 00
Rent Expense	4 0 0 00	
Utilities Expense	2 0 0 00	
Totals	$12 7 0 0 00	$12 7 0 0 00

PROBLEM 2A-4 OR PROBLEM 2B-4

(A)

GRACIE LANTZ, ATTORNEY AT LAW
INCOME STATEMENT
FOR MONTH ENDED MAY 31, 19XX

Revenue:								$1	3	5 0	00
Legal Fees											
Operating Expenses											
Utilities Expense		$	3 0	0	00						
Rent Expense			4 5	0	00						
Salary Expense			1 5	0	00						
Total Operating Expenses									9 0	0	00
Net Income								$	4 5	0	00

(B)

GRACIE LANTZ, ATTORNEY AT LAW
STATEMENT OF OWNER'S EQUITY
FOR MONTH ENDED MAY 31, 19XX

G. Lantz, Capital May 31, 19XX								$1	2 7	5	00
Net Income for May		$	4 5	0	00						
Less Withdrawal for May			3 0	0	00						
Increase in Capital									1 5	0	00
G. Lantz, Capital May 31, 19XX								$ 1	4 2	5	00

43

PROBLEM 2A-4 OR 2B-4 (CONCLUDED)

(C)

GRACIE LANTZ, ATTORNEY AT LAW
BALANCE SHEET
MAY 31, 19XX

ASSETS			LIABILITIES AND OWNER'S EQUITY		
Cash	$5000 00		Liabilities		
Account Recievable	650 00		Accounts Payable	$4300 00
Office Equipment	750 00		Salary Payable	675 00
			Owner's Equity		
			G. Lantz, Capital	1425 00
Total Assets	6400 00		Total Liabilities and	$6400 00
			Owner's Equity		

PROBLEM 2A-5 OR PROBLEM 2B-5

(1,2,3)

Cash 111	Accounts Payable 211	Advertising Expense 511

Accounts Receivable 112	A. Angel, Capital 311	Gas Expense 512

Office Equipment 121	A. Angel, Withdrawals 312	Salaries Expense 513

Delivery Trucks 122	Delivery Fees Earned 411	Telephone Expense 514

ANGEL'S DELIVERY SERVICE
TRIAL BALANCE
MARCH 31,19XX

		Dr.		Cr.	

ANGEL'S DELIVERY SERVICE
INCOME STATEMENT
FOR MONTH ENDED MARCH 31, 19XX

(5B)

ANGEL'S DELIVERY SERVICE
STATEMENT OF OWNER'S EQUITY
FOR MONTH ENDED MARCH 31, 19XX

(5C)

ANGEL'S DELIVERY SERVICE
BALANCE SHEET
MARCH 31, 19XX

ASSETS			LIABILITIES AND OWNER'S EQUITY		

CHAPTER 2
SUMMARY PRACTICE TEST:
DEBITS AND CREDITS: ANALYZING AND RECORDING
BUSINESS TRANSACTIONS

Part I Instructions

Fill in the blank(s) to complete the statement.

1. _____ accumulate information in a book called the ledger.
2. The left side of any T account is called the _____ _____.
3. Assets are increased by _____.
4. The process of balancing an account involves _____.
5. Transaction anaylsis charts are an aid in recoding _____ _____.
6. The _____ _____ _____ indicates the names and numbering system of accounts.
7. A _____ is a group of accounts.
8. A _____ _____ is an informal report that lists accounts and their balances.
9. Withdrawals are increased by _____.
10. The income statement, statement of owner's equity, and balance sheet may be prepared from a _____ _____.
11. Cash, Accounts Receivable, and Equipment are examples of _____.
12. Increasing expenses ultimately cause owner's equity to _____.
13. An increase in rent expense is a _____ by the rules of debits and credits.
14. A debit to one asset and a credit to another asset for the same transaction reflect a _____ in assets.
15. The category of accounts payable is a/an_____.

Part II Instructions

Abby Lane opened a taxi company. From the following chart of accounts, indicate in column B (by account number) which account (s) will be debited or credited as related to the transaction in column A.

Chart of Accounts

ASSETS	LIABILITIES	EXPENSES
10 Cash	50 Accounts Payable	80 Advertising
20 Accounts Receivable		90 Gas
30 Equipment	OWNER'S EQUITY	100 Salaries
40 Taxi	60 A. Lane, Capital	110 Telephone
	62 A. Lane, Withdrawals	
	REVENUE	
	70 Taxi Fees Earned	

COLUMN A

COLUMN B

		DEBIT(S)	CREDIT(S)
1.	EXAMPLE: Abby Lane invested $25,000 in the taxi company.	10	60
2.	Purchased a taxi on account for $40,000.		
3.	Bought equipment on account for $6,000.		
4.	Advertising bill received, but not paid til next month.		
5.	Abby paid home telephone bill from company checkbook, $20.		
6.	Collected $100 in cash from daily taxi fees earned.		
7.	Customer charged a taxi ride of $10.		
8.	Received partial payment for Transaction #7 of $5.		
9.	Paid business telephone bill, $32.		
10.	Purchased additional equipment for cash, $550.		
11.	Paid taxi driver salaries of $150.		
12.	Drove customer on account to local train station for $6.		
13.	Received $5 from customer who hired taxi for ride across town.		
14.	Collected from past charged revenue, $15.		
15.	Bought office equipment on account for $110.		

Part III Instructions

Answer true or false to the following statements.

1. There are debit and credit columns found on the three financial reports.
2. A trial balance could balance but be wrong.
3. Withdrawals are listed on the credit column of the trial balance.
4. Double entry bookkeeping results in a system where the sum of all the debits is equal to the sum of all the credits.
5. The ledger is numbered like a textbook.

6. Withdrawals are always increased by credits.

7. An expense could create a liability.

8. A shift in assets means the total of assets must change.

9. The rules of debit and credit are constantly changing.

10. The transaction analysis chart is a teaching device.

11. The chart of accounts helps locating and identifying accounts quickly.

12. The left side of any account is a credit.

13. A debit means all accounts are decreasing.

14. Financial reports are prepared from a trial balance.

15. The statement of owner's equity is prepared before the income statement.

16. Liabilities increase by credits.

17. Footings aid in balancing accounts.

18. Withdrawals are listed on the income statement.

19. The balance sheet contains the old figure for capital.

20. Think of a credit as always meaning something good.

CHAPTER 2
SOLUTIONS TO SUMMARY PRACTICE TEST

Part I

1.	accounts	6.	chart of accounts	11.	assets
2.	debit side	7.	ledger (general)	12.	decrease
3.	debits	8.	trial balance	13.	debit
4.	footings	9.	debits	14.	shift
5.	business transactions	10.	trial balance	15.	liability

Part II

	Debit	Credit			Debit	Credit			Debit	Credit
1	10	60		6.	10	70		11.	100	10
2.	40	50		7.	20	70		12.	20	70
3.	30	50		8.	10	20		13.	10	70
4.	80	50		9.	110	10		14.	10	20
5.	62	10		10.	30	10		15.	30	50

Part III

1.	false	6.	false	11.	true	16.	true
2.	true	7.	true	12.	false	17.	true
3.	false	8.	false	13.	false	18.	false
4.	true	9.	false	14.	true	19.	false
5.	false	10.	true	15.	false	20.	false

CHAPTERS 1-2
ACCOUNTING RECALL FORMS

Part I   **Part II**

1. _____   6. _____   11. _____
2. _____   7. _____   12. _____
3. _____   8. _____   13. _____
4. _____   9. _____   14. _____
5. _____   10. _____   15. _____

Name Lauren Peterson   Class Accounting   Date Oct. 9

CONTINUING PROBLEM FOR CHAPTER 2

Computer Shop Equipment 1080
Bal. 1,200

Freedman, Capital 3000
4,500 Bal.

Rent Expense 5020
Bal. 400

Insurance Expense 5060
(L) 150

Supplies 1030
Bal. 250
(S) 200
450

Accounts Payable 2000
(m) 200 | 335 Bal.
          200 (S)
          535
          200
          535

Advertising Expense 5010
(N) 1,400

Supplies Expense 5050

Accounts Receivable 1020
(O) 850

Office Equipment 1090
Bal. 600

Service Revenue 4000
(P) 900 | 1,650 Bal.
           850 (O)
           2,500
           900
           1,600 (g)

Phone Expense 5040
(K) 155

Cash 1000
Bal. 3,850 | 155 (K)
(P) 900 | 150 (L)
           | 200 (m)
           | 1,400 (N)
           | 85 (B)
           | 50 (R)
4,750   2,040
-2,040
2,710

Freedman, Withdrawals 3010
Bal. 100

Utilities Expense 5030
Bal. 85
(Q) 85
170

Postage Expense 5070
(R) 50

ELDORADO COMPUTER CENTER
TRIAL BALANCE
AUGUST 31, 19XX

	Dr.	Cr.
Cash	$2 7 1 0 00	
Accounts Receivable	8 5 0 00	
Supplies	4 5 0 00	
Computer Shop Equipment	1 2 0 0 00	
Office Equipment	6 0 0 00	
Accounts Payable		$3 3 5 00
Freedman, Capital		4 5 0 0 00
Freedman, Withdrawal	1 0 0 00	
Service Revenue		1 6 0 0 00
Advertising Expense	1 4 0 0 00	
Rent Expense	4 0 0 00	
Utilities Expense	1 7 0 00	
Phone Expense	1 5 5 00	
Insurance Expense	1 5 0 00	
Postage Expense	5 0 00	
Totals		

ELDORADO COMPUTER CENTER
INCOME STATEMENT
FOR THE TWO MONTHS ENDED AUGUST 31, 19XX

ELDORADO COMPUTER CENTER
STATEMENT OF OWNER'S EQUITY
FOR THE TWO MONTHS ENDED AUGUST 31, 19XX

ELDORADO COMPUTER CENTER
BALANCE SHEET
AUGUST 31, 19XX

ASSETS				LIABILITIES AND OWNER'S EQUITY			

SOLUTIONS TO ACCOUNTING RECALL

Part I

1. J	**6.** G
2. F	**7.** A
3. I	**8.** E
4. H	**9.** D
5. B	**10.** C

Part II

11. False; (depends on category)

12. True

13. False; (Beg. figure) It is the calculation of capital from statement of owner's equity that goes on the balance sheet.

14. False; (Debit)

15. True

BEGINNING THE ACCOUNTING CYCLE: JOURNALIZING, POSTING, AND THE TRIAL BALANCE

3

SELF-REVIEW QUIZ 3-1

LOWE'S REPAIR SERVICE
GENERAL JOURNAL

PAGE 1

Date	Account Titles and Description	PR	Dr.	Cr.

LOWE'S REPAIR SERVICE
GENERAL JOURNAL

PAGE 1 (cont'd)

Date	Account Titles and Description	PR	Dr.	Cr.

SELF-REVIEW QUIZ 3-2

CLARK'S WORD PROCESSING SERVICES
GENERAL JOURNAL

PAGE 1

Date 19xx		Account Titles and Description	PR	Dr.					Cr.				
May	1	Cash		10	0	0	0	00					
		Brenda Clark, Capital							10	0	0	0	00
		Initial investment of cash by owner											
	1	Word Processing Equipment		6	0	0	0	00					
		Cash							1	0	0	0	00
		Accounts Payable							5	0	0	0	00
		Purchase of equip. from Ben Co.											
	1	Prepaid Rent		1	2	0	0	00					
		Cash							1	2	0	0	00
		Rent paid in advance (3 months)											
	3	Office Supplies			6	0	0	00					
		Accounts Payable								6	0	0	00
		Purchase of supplies on acct. from Norris											
	7	Cash		3	0	0	0	00					
		Word Processing Fees							3	0	0	0	00
		Cash received for services rendered											
	15	Office Salaries Expense			6	5	0	00					
		Cash								6	5	0	00
		Payment of office salaries											
	18	Advertising Expense			2	5	0	00					
		Accounts Payable								2	5	0	00
		Bill received but not paid from Al's News											
	20	Brenda Clark, Withdrawals			6	2	5	00					
		Cash								6	2	5	00
		Personal withdrawal of cash											
	22	Accounts Receivable		5	0	0	0	00					
		Word Processing Fees							5	0	0	0	00
		Billed Morris Co. for fees earned											

CLARK'S WORD PROCESSING SERVICES
GENERAL JOURNAL

PAGE 2

Date 19xx		Account Titles and Description	PR	Dr.					Cr.				
May	27	Office Salaries Expense			6	5	0	00					
		Cash									6	5	0	00
		Payment of office salaries											
	28	Accounts Payable		2	5	0	0	00					
		Cash								2	5	0	0	00
		Paid half the amount owed Ben Co.											
	29	Telephone Expense			2	2	0	00					
		Cash									2	2	0	00
		Paid telephone bill											

PARTIAL LEDGER OF CLARK'S WORD PROCESSING SERVICE

CASH   ACCOUNT NO. 111

Date	Explanation	Post Ref.	Debit	Credit	Balance	
					Debit	Credit

ACCOUNTS RECEIVABLE   ACCOUNT NO. 112

Date	Explanation	Post Ref.	Debit	Credit	Balance	
					Debit	Credit

OFFICE SUPPLIES   ACCOUNT NO. 114

Date	Explanation	Post Ref.	Debit	Credit	Balance Debit	Balance Credit

PREPAID RENT   ACCOUNT NO. 115

Date	Explanation	Post Ref.	Debit	Credit	Balance Debit	Balance Credit

WORD PROCESSING EQUIPMENT   ACCOUNT NO. 121

Date	Explanation	Post Ref.	Debit	Credit	Balance Debit	Balance Credit

ACCOUNTS PAYABLE   ACCOUNT NO. 211

Date	Explanation	Post Ref.	Debit	Credit	Balance Debit	Balance Credit

BRENDA CLARK, CAPITAL   ACCOUNT NO. 311

Date	Explanation	Post Ref.	Debit	Credit	Balance Debit	Balance Credit

BRENDA CLARK, WITHDRAWALS   ACCOUNT NO. 312

Date	Explanation	Post Ref.	Debit	Credit	Balance Debit	Balance Credit

WORD PROCESSING FEES   ACCOUNT NO. 411

Date	Explanation	Post Ref.	Debit	Credit	Balance Debit	Balance Credit

OFFICE SALARIES EXPENSE   ACCOUNT NO. 511

Date	Explanation	Post Ref.	Debit	Credit	Balance Debit	Balance Credit

ADVERTISING EXPENSE   ACCOUNT NO. 512

Date	Explanation	Post Ref.	Debit	Credit	Balance Debit	Balance Credit

TELEPHONE EXPENSE   ACCOUNT NO. 513

Date	Explanation	Post Ref.	Debit	Credit	Balance Debit	Balance Credit

SELF-REVIEW QUIZ 3-3

1. _____

_____

_____

2.   P. 4

Date		Account Titles and Description	PR		Dr.			Cr.		

FORMS FOR COMPREHENSIVE DEMONSTRATION PROBLEM
(A,B)

**ABBY'S EMPLOYMENT AGENCY
GENERAL JOURNAL**

PAGE 1

Date	Account Titles and Description	PR	Dr.	Cr.

FORMS FOR COMPREHENSIVE DEMONSTRATION PROBLEM (CONTINUED)

GENERAL LEDGER OF ABBY'S PLACEMENT AGENCY

CASH   ACCOUNT NO. 111

Date	Explanation	Post Ref.	Debit	Credit	Balance Debit	Balance Credit

ACCOUNTS RECEIVABLE   ACCOUNT NO. 112

Date	Explanation	Post Ref.	Debit	Credit	Balance Debit	Balance Credit

SUPPLIES   ACCOUNT NO. 131

Date	Explanation	Post Ref.	Debit	Credit	Balance Debit	Balance Credit

EQUIPMENT   ACCOUNT NO. 141

Date	Explanation	Post Ref.	Debit	Credit	Balance Debit	Balance Credit

FORMS FOR COMPREHENSIVE DEMONSTRATION PROBLEM (CONTINUED)

ACCOUNTS PAYABLE — ACCOUNT NO. 211

Date	Explanation	Post Ref.	Debit	Credit	Balance Debit	Balance Credit

A. TODD, CAPITAL — ACCOUNT NO. 311

Date	Explanation	Post Ref.	Debit	Credit	Balance Debit	Balance Credit

A. TODD, WITHDRAWALS — ACCOUNT NO. 321

Date	Explanation	Post Ref.	Debit	Credit	Balance Debit	Balance Credit

EMPLOYMENT FEES EARNED — ACCOUNT NO. 411

Date	Explanation	Post Ref.	Debit	Credit	Balance Debit	Balance Credit

FORMS FOR COMPREHENSIVE DEMONSTRATION PROBLEM (CONTINUED)

WAGE EXPENSE **ACCOUNT NO. 511**

Date	Explanation	Post Ref.	Debit	Credit	Balance	
					Debit	Credit

TELEPHONE EXPENSE **ACCOUNT NO. 521**

Date	Explanation	Post Ref.	Debit	Credit	Balance	
					Debit	Credit

ADVERTISING EXPENSE **ACCOUNT NO. 531**

Date	Explanation	Post Ref.	Debit	Credit	Balance	
					Debit	Credit

Name_____ Class _____ Date _____

FORMS FOR COMPREHENSIVE DEMONSTRATION PROBLEM (CONTINUED)

ABBY'S EMPLOYMENT AGENCY
TRIAL BALANCE
MARCH 31, 19XX

		Dr.		Cr.

YOU MAKE THE CALL: CRITICAL THINKING/ETHICAL CASE

_____
_____
_____
_____
_____
_____
_____
_____
_____
_____
_____
_____
_____
_____
_____
_____
_____
_____
_____
_____
_____
_____
_____
_____
_____
_____
_____
_____
_____
_____
_____
_____
_____
_____
_____
_____
_____
_____
_____
_____
_____
_____
_____
_____

CHAPTER 3
FORMS FOR MINI EXERCISES

1. A. _____   E. _____
   B. _____   F. _____
   C. _____   G. _____
   D. _____   H. _____
                           I. _____

2. A. _____
   B. _____
   C. _____

3. _____

   _____

4.

LARKIN CO.
TRIAL BALANCE
OCTOBER 31, 19XX

		Dr.	Cr.

5.

FORMS FOR EXERCISES

3-1.

Date		Account Titles and Description	PR		Dr.				Cr.			

3-2.

Date	Account Titles and Description	PR	Dr.	Cr.

Name_____ Class _____ Date _____

EXERCISES (CONTINUED)

3-3.   P. 4

Date		Account Titles and Description	PR	Dr.					Cr.				
April	6	Cash		15	0	0	0	—					
		A. King, Capital							15	0	0	0	—
		Cash investment											
	14	Equipment		9	0	0	0	—					
		Cash							4	0	0	0	—
		Accounts Payable							5	0	0	0	—
		Purchase of Equipment											

CASH   ACCOUNT NO. 111

Date	Explanation	Post Ref.	Debit	Credit	Balance Debit	Balance Credit

EQUIPMENT   ACCOUNT NO. 121

Date	Explanation	Post Ref.	Debit	Credit	Balance Debit	Balance Credit

ACCOUNTS PAYABLE   ACCOUNT NO. 211

Date	Explanation	Post Ref.	Debit	Credit	Balance Debit	Balance Credit

A. KING, CAPITAL   ACCOUNT NO. 311

Date	Explanation	Post Ref.	Debit	Credit	Balance Debit	Balance Credit

EXERCISES (CONTINUED)

3-4.

(A)   PAGE 1

Date	Account Titles and Description	PR	Dr.	Cr.

(B)

CASH   ACCOUNT NO. 111

Date	Explanation	Post Ref.	Debit	Credit	Balance Debit	Balance Credit

ACCOUNTS RECEIVABLE   ACCOUNT NO. 112

Date	Explanation	Post Ref.	Debit	Credit	Balance Debit	Balance Credit

EXERCISES (CONTINUED)

EQUIPMENT   ACCOUNT NO. 121

Date	Explanation	Post Ref.	Debit	Credit	Balance Debit	Balance Credit

ACCOUNTS PAYABLE   ACCOUNT NO. 211

Date	Explanation	Post Ref.	Debit	Credit	Balance Debit	Balance Credit

J. LOWE, CAPITAL   ACCOUNT NO. 311

Date	Explanation	Post Ref.	Debit	Credit	Balance Debit	Balance Credit

J. LOWE, WITHDRAWALS   ACCOUNT NO. 312

Date	Explanation	Post Ref.	Debit	Credit	Balance Debit	Balance Credit

FEES EARNED   ACCOUNT NO. 411

Date	Explanation	Post Ref.	Debit	Credit	Balance Debit	Balance Credit

SALARIES EXPENSE   ACCOUNT NO. 511

Date	Explanation	Post Ref.	Debit	Credit	Balance Debit	Balance Credit

EXERCISES (CONTINUED)

(C)

LOWE COMPANY
TRIAL BALANCE
JULY 31, 19XX

		Dr.		Cr.

3-5.

SUNG CO.
TRIAL BALANCE
MARCH 31, 19XX

		Dr.		Cr.

3-6.

		Dr.		Cr.

END OF CHAPTER PROBLEMS

PROBLEM 3A-1 OR PROBLEM 3B-1

VANCE'S DOG GROOMING CENTER
GENERAL JOURNAL

PAGE 1

Date		Account Titles and Description	PR	Dr.	Cr.
19XX					
July	1	Prepaid Rent		3 0 0 0 00	
		Cash			3 0 0 0 00
	3	Grooming Equipment		2 5 0 0 00	
		Accounts Payable			2 5 0 0 00
	12	Cash		1 4 0 0 00	
		Fees Earned			1 4 0 0 00
	10	Grooming Supplies		6 0 0 00	
		Cash			6 0 0 00
	20	S. Vance, Withdrawal		4 0 0 00	
		Cash			4 0 0 00
	21	Advertising Expense		1 2 0 00	
		Accounts Payable			1 2 0 00
	25	Cleaning Expense		9 0 00	
		Cash			9 0 00
	28	Salaries Expense		5 0 0 00	
		Cash			5 0 0 00
	29	Accounts Receivable		1 7 0 0 00	
		Grooming Fees Earned			1 7 0 0 00
	30	Accounts Payable		1 2 5 0 00	
		Cash			1 2 5 0 00
		Totals		$ 11 5 6 0 00	$ 11 5 6 0 00

PROBLEM 3A-1 OR PROBLEM 3B-1 (CONTINUED)

VANCE'S DOG GROOMING CENTER
GENERAL JOURNAL

Date 19xx		Account Titles and Description	PR	Dr.	Cr.

PROBLEM 3A-2 OR PROBLEM 3B-2
(A,B)

TAYLOR'S DANCE STUDIO
GENERAL JOURNAL

PAGE 1

Date		Account Titles and Description	PR	Dr.	Cr.
19XX					
June	1	Cash	111	$8 0 0 0 00	
		M. Taylor, Capital	311		$8 0 0 0 00
	1	Prepaid Rent	114	1 0 0 0 00	
		Cash	111		1 0 0 0 00
	3	Office Equipment	131	7 0 0 00	
		Accounts Payable	211		7 0 0 00
	5	Cash	111	9 0 0 00	
		Fees Earned	411		9 0 0 00
	8	Supplies	121	3 0 0 00	
		Cash	111		3 0 0 00
	9	Accounts Receivable	112	2 1 0 0 00	
		Fees Earned	411		2 1 0 0 00
	10	Salaries Expense	512	4 0 0 00	
		Cash	111		4 0 0 00
	15	M. Taylor, Withdrawal	312	1 5 0 00	
		Cash	111		1 5 0 00
	28	Electrical Expense	511	1 2 5 00	
		Cash	111		1 2 5 00
	29	Telephone Expense	531	1 9 0 00	
		Cash	111		1 9 0 00
		Totals		$13 8 6 5 00	$13 8 6 5 00

PROBLEM 3A-2 OR PROBLEM 3B-2(CONTINUED)

GENERAL LEDGER OF TAYLOR'S DANCE STUDIO

CASH — ACCOUNT NO. 111

Date	Explanation	Post Ref.	Debit	Credit	Balance Debit	Balance Credit
19XX June 1		G.J.1	8 000 00		8 000 00	
1		G.J.1		1 000 00	7 000 00	
5		G.J.1	9 00 00		7 900 00	
8		G.J.1		3 00 00	7 600 00	
10		G.J.1		4 00 00	7 200 00	
15		G.J.1		1 50 00	7 050 00	
28		G.J.1		1 25 00	6 925 00	
29		G.J.1		1 90 00	6 735 00	

ACCOUNTS RECEIVABLE — ACCOUNT NO. 112

Date	Explanation	Post Ref.	Debit	Credit	Balance Debit	Balance Credit
19XX June 9		G.J.1	2 100 00		2 100 00	

PREPAID RENT — ACCOUNT NO. 114

Date	Explanation	Post Ref.	Debit	Credit	Balance Debit	Balance Credit
19XX June 1		G.J.1	1 000 00		1 000 00	

SUPPLIES — ACCOUNT NO. 121

Date	Explanation	Post Ref.	Debit	Credit	Balance Debit	Balance Credit
19XX June 8		G.J.1	3 00 00		3 00 00	

PROBLEM 3A-2 OR PROBLEM 3B-2 (CONTINUED)

EQUIPMENT   ACCOUNT NO. 131

Date	Explanation	Post Ref.	Debit	Credit	Balance Debit	Balance Credit
19XX June 3		G.J.1	70000		70000	

ACCOUNTS PAYABLE   ACCOUNT NO. 211

Date	Explanation	Post Ref.	Debit	Credit	Balance Debit	Balance Credit
19XX June 3		G.J.1		70000		70000

MOLLY TAYLOR, CAPITAL   ACCOUNT NO. 311

Date	Explanation	Post Ref.	Debit	Credit	Balance Debit	Balance Credit
19XX June 1		G.J.1		80000		80000

MOLLY TAYLOR, WITHDRAWALS   ACCOUNT NO. 312

Date	Explanation	Post Ref.	Debit	Credit	Balance Debit	Balance Credit
19XX June 15		G.J.1	150		15000	

PROBLEM 3A-2 OR PROBLEM 3B-2 (CONTINUED)

FEES EARNED   ACCOUNT NO. 411

Date		Explanation	Post Ref.	Debit	Credit	Balance Debit	Balance Credit
19XX June	5		G.J.1		900 00		900 00
	9		G.J.1		2100 00		3000 00

ELECTRICAL EXPENSE   ACCOUNT NO. 511

Date		Explanation	Post Ref.	Debit	Credit	Balance Debit	Balance Credit
19XX June	28		G.J.1	125 00		125 00	

SALARIES EXPENSE   ACCOUNT NO. 512

Date		Explanation	Post Ref.	Debit	Credit	Balance Debit	Balance Credit
19XX June	10		G.J.1	400 00		400 00	

TELEPHONE EXPENSE   ACCOUNT NO. 531

Date		Explanation	Post Ref.	Debit	Credit	Balance Debit	Balance Credit
19XX June	29		G.J.1	190 00		190 00	

PROBLEM 3A-2 OR PROBLEM 3B-2 (CONCLUDED)

(C)

TAYLOR'S DANCE STUDIO
TRIAL BALANCE
JUNE 30, 19XX

	Dr.	Cr.
Cash	$6 735 00	
Accounts Receivable	2 10 00	
Prepaid Rent	1 00 00	
Supplies	3 00 00	
Equipment	7 00 00	
Accounts Payable		$ 7 00 00
M. Taylor, Capital		8 00 00
M. Taylor, Withdrawal	1 50 00	
Fees Earned		3 00 00
Electrical Expense	1 25 00	
Salaries Expense	4 00 00	
Telephone Expense	1 90 00	
Totals	$11 7 00 00	$11 7 00 00

PROBLEM 3A-3 OR PROBLEM 3B-3
(A,B)

A. FRENCH'S PLACEMENT AGENCY
GENERAL JOURNAL

P. 1

Date		Account Titles and Description	PR	Dr.					Cr.				
19xx													
June	1	Cash	111	$9	0	0	0	00					
		A. French, Capital	311						$9	0	0	0	00
	1	Equipment	141	2	0	0	0	00					
		Account Payable	211						2	0	0	0	00
	3	Account Receivable	112	1	6	0	0	00					
		Placement Fees Earned	411						1	6	0	0	00
	5	A. French, Withdrawal	312		1	0	0	00					
		Cash	111							1	0	0	00
	7	Wage Expense	511		3	0	0	00					
		Cash	111							3	0	0	00
	9	Cash	111		6	0	0	00					
		Placement Fees Earned	411							6	0	0	00
	15	Supplies	131		5	0	0	00					
		Account Payable	211							5	0	0	00
	28	Telephone Expense	521		1	6	0	00					
		Cash	111							1	6	0	00
	29	Advertising Expense	531		9	0	0	00					
		Account Payable	211							9	0	0	00
		Totals		$15	1	6	0	00	$15	1	6	0	00

PROBLEM 3A-3 OR PROBLEM 3B-3

PROBLEM 3A-3 OR PROBLEM 3B-3 (CONTINUED)

GENERAL LEDGER OF A. FRENCH'S PLACEMENT AGENCY

CASH
ACCOUNT NO. 111

Date	Explanation	Post Ref.	Debit	Credit	Balance Debit	Balance Credit
19XX						
June 1		G.J.1	9 000 00		9 000 00	
5		G.J.1		1 000 00	8 900 00	
7		G.J.1		300 00	8 600 00	
9		G.J.1	600 00		9 200 00	
28				160 00	9 040 00	

ACCOUNTS RECEIVABLE
ACCOUNT NO. 112

Date	Explanation	Post Ref.	Debit	Credit	Balance Debit	Balance Credit
19XX						
June 3		G.J.1	1 600 00		1 600 00	

SUPPLIES
ACCOUNT NO. 131

Date	Explanation	Post Ref.	Debit	Credit	Balance Debit	Balance Credit
19XX						
June 15		G.J.1	500 00		500 00	

EQUIPMENT
ACCOUNT NO. 141

Date	Explanation	Post Ref.	Debit	Credit	Balance Debit	Balance Credit
19XX						
June 1		G.J.1	2 000 00		2 000 00	

PROBLEM 3A-3 OR PROBLEM 3B-3 (CONTINUED)

ACCOUNTS PAYABLE   **ACCOUNT NO. 211**

Date	Explanation	Post Ref.	Debit	Credit	Balance Debit	Balance Credit
19XX June 1		G.J.1		2 0 0 0 00		2 0 0 0 00
15		G.J.1		5 0 0 00		2 5 0 0 00
29		G.J.1		9 0 0 00		3 4 0 0 00

A. FRENCH, CAPITAL   **ACCOUNT NO. 311**

Date	Explanation	Post Ref.	Debit	Credit	Balance Debit	Balance Credit
19XX June 1		G.J.1		9 0 0 0 00		9 0 0 0 00

A. FRENCH, WITHDRAWALS   **ACCOUNT NO. 312**

Date	Explanation	Post Ref.	Debit	Credit	Balance Debit	Balance Credit
19XX June 5		G.J.1	1 0 0 00		1 0 0 00	

PLACEMENT FEES EARNED   **ACCOUNT NO. 411**

Date	Explanation	Post Ref.	Debit	Credit	Balance Debit	Balance Credit
19XX June 3		G.J.1		1 6 0 0 00		1 6 0 0 00
9		G.J.1		6 0 0 00		2 2 0 0 00

PROBLEM 3A-3 OR PROBLEM 3B-3 (CONTINUED)

WAGE EXPENSE   ACCOUNT NO. 511

Date	Explanation	Post Ref.	Debit	Credit	Balance Debit	Balance Credit
19XX June 7		G.J.1	300 00		300 00	

TELEPHONE EXPENSE   ACCOUNT NO. 521

Date	Explanation	Post Ref.	Debit	Credit	Balance Debit	Balance Credit
19XX June 28		G.J.1	160 00		160 00	

ADVERTISING EXPENSE   ACCOUNT NO. 531

Date	Explanation	Post Ref.	Debit	Credit	Balance Debit	Balance Credit
19XX June 29		G.J.1	900 00		900 00	

PROBLEM 3A-3 OR PROBLEM 3B-3 (CONTINUED)

(C)

A. FRENCH'S PLACEMENT AGENCY
TRIAL BALANCE
JUNE 30, 19XX

	Dr.	Cr.
Cash	$9 0 4 0 00	
Account Receivable	1 6 0 0 00	
Supplies	5 0 0 00	
Equipment	2 0 0 0 00	
Account Payable		$3 4 0 0 00
A. French, Capital		9 0 0 0 00
A. French, Withdrawal	1 0 0 0 00	
Placement Fees Earned		2 2 0 0 00
Wage Expense	3 0 0 00	
Telephone Expense	1 6 0 00	
Advertising Expense	9 0 00	
Totals	$14 6 0 0 00	$14 6 0 0 00

CHAPTER 3
SUMMARY PRACTICE TEST:
BEGINNING THE ACCOUNTING CYCLE: JOURNALIZING, POSTING, AND THE TRIAL BALANCE

1. A _____ _____ is an accounting period that runs for any 12 consecutive months.

2. _____ _____ are prepared for parts of a fiscal year (monthly, quarterly, etc.).

3. The _____ _____ _____ eliminates the need for footings.

4. The positive balance of each account is referred to as its _____ _____.

5. The process of recording transactions in a journal is called _____.

6. Entries are journalized in _____ _____.

7. A ledger is often called a _____ _____ _____ _____.

8. The _____ portion of a journal entry is indented and placed below the _____ portion.

9. A journal entry requiring three or more accounts is called a _____ _____ _____.

10. Prepaid rent is a(n) _____ on the balance sheet.

11. When supplies are used up or consumed they become a(n) _____.

12. The book of original entry usually refers to a(n) _____.

13. The process of transferring information from a journal to a ledger is called _____.

14. _____ deals with the process of updating the PR of the journal from the account number of the ledger to indicate to which account in the ledger information has been posted.

15. Recording $885.000 as $88.50 is an example of a _____.

Part II Instructions

Match the term in column A to the definition, example, or phrase in column B. Be sure to use a letter only once.

COLUMN A

___g___ 1. EXAMPLE: Book of original entry
_____ 2. Withdrawals
_____ 3. Slide
_____ 4. Transposition
_____ 5. Posting
_____ 6. General Journal
_____ 7. Cross-reference
_____ 8. Journalizing
_____ 9. Balance Sheet prepared monthly
_____10. A fiscal year

COLUMN B

a. 118 — 1180
b. Transferring information from a general journal to a ledger
c. Chronological order
d. Increased by a credit
e. Non-business expense
f. Compound journal entry
g. General journal
h. Rearrangement of digits of a number by accident
i. Updating PR column of journal from ledger account
j. Trial balance
k. Place to record transactions
l. Accounting cycle
m. Accounting period
n. Interim reports

Part III Instructions

Answer true or false to the following statements.

1. 5,187 written by mistake as 5,178 is an example of a slide.
2. The totals of a trial balance may possibly not balance due to transpositions.
3. Withdrawals has a normal balance of a credit.
4. The running balance of an account can be kept in a four-column account.
5. The journal links debits and credits in alphabetical order.
6. The ledger accumulates information from the journal.
7. The post reference column of a ledger records the account number of that account.
8. An accounting cycle must be from January 1 to December 31.
9. The ledger is the book of original entry.
10. The income statement is prepared for a specific accounting period.
11. Interim reports are prepared for an entire fiscal year.
12. A calendar year could be a fiscal year.
13. 150 written by mistake as 1,500 is an example of a slide.

14. If the totals of a trial balance balance, the individual balance of items must be correct.
15. The equality of debits and credits on a trial balance does not guarantee that transactions have been properly recorded.
16. The trial balance is prepared from the journal.
17. Cross-referencing means never updating the post reference column of the journal.
18. Journals and ledgers are always in the same book.
19. The normal balance of each account is located on the same side that increases the acccount.
20. Ruling of four-column accounts is eliminated.

CHAPTER 3
SOLUTIONS TO SUMMARY PRACTICE TEST

Part I

1. fiscal year
2. interim reports
3. four-column
4. normal balance
5. journalizing

6. chronological order
7. book of final entry
8. credit, debit
9. compound journal
10. asset

11. expense
12. journal
13. posting
14. cross-reference
15. slide

Part II

1. g
2. e
3. a
4. h
5. b

6. k
7. i
8. c
9. n
10. m

Part III

1. false
2. true
3. false
4. true
5. false

6. true
7. false
8. false
9. false
10. true

11. false
12. true
13. true
14. false
15. true

16. false
17. false
18. false
19. true
20. true

CHAPTERS 1-3
ACCOUNTING RECALL FORMS

Part I

1. _____

2. _____

3. _____

4. _____

5. _____

6. _____

7. _____

8. _____

9. _____

10. _____

Part II

11. _____

12. _____

13. _____

14. _____

15. _____

CONTINUING PROBLEM FOR CHAPTER 3

ELDORADO COMPUTER CENTER
GENERAL JOURNAL

PAGE 1

Date	Account Titles and Description	PR	Dr.	Cr.

ELDORADO COMPUTER CENTER
GENERAL JOURNAL

PAGE 1 (Cont.)

Date	Account Titles and Description	PR	Dr.	Cr.

CASH   **ACCOUNT NO. 1000**

Date		Explanation	Post Ref.	Debit					Credit					Balance Debit					Credit				
9/1	XX	Balance forward	√											2	8	6	5	00					

ACCOUNTS RECEIVABLE   ACCOUNT NO. 1020

Date		Explanation	Post Ref.	Debit	Credit	Balance Debit	Balance Credit
9/1	XX	Balance Forward	√			8 5 0 00	

PREPAID RENT   ACCOUNT NO. 1025

Date	Explanation	Post Ref.	Debit	Credit	Balance Debit	Balance Credit

SUPPLIES   ACCOUNT NO. 1030

Date		Explanation	Post Ref.	Debit	Credit	Balance Debit	Balance Credit
9/1	XX	Balance forward	√			4 5 0 00	

COMPUTER SHOP EQUIPMENT   ACCOUNT NO. 1080

Date		Explanation	Post Ref.	Debit	Credit	Balance Debit	Balance Credit
9/1	XX		√			1 2 0 0 00	

Name_____ Class _____ Date _____

OFFICE EQUIPMENT   ACCOUNT NO. 1090

Date		Explanation	Post Ref.	Debit	Credit	Balance Debit	Balance Credit
9/1	XX	Balance forward	√			6 0 0 00	

ACCOUNTS PAYABLE   ACCOUNT NO. 2000

Date		Explanation	Post Ref.	Debit	Credit	Balance Debit	Balance Credit
9/1	XX	Balance forward	√				4 0 5 00

FREEDMAN, CAPITAL   ACCOUNT NO. 3000

Date		Explanation	Post Ref.	Debit	Credit	Balance Debit	Balance Credit
9/1	XX	Balance forward	√				4 5 0 0 00

FREEDMAN, WITHDRAWALS   ACCOUNT NO. 3010

Date		Explanation	Post Ref.	Debit	Credit	Balance Debit	Balance Credit
9/1	XX	Balance forward	√			1 0 0 00	

SERVICE REVENUE   ACCOUNT NO. 4000

Date		Explanation	Post Ref.	Debit	Credit	Balance	
						Debit	Credit
9/1	XX	Balance forward	√				3 4 0 0 00

ADVERTISING EXPENSE   ACCOUNT NO. 5010

Date		Explanation	Post Ref.	Debit	Credit	Balance	
						Debit	Credit
9/1	XX	Balance forward	√			1 4 0 0 00	

RENT EXPENSE   ACCOUNT NO. 5020

Date		Explanation	Post Ref.	Debit	Credit	Balance	
						Debit	Credit
9/1	XX	Balance forward	√			4 0 0 00	

UTILITIES EXPENSE   ACCOUNT NO. 5030

Date		Explanation	Post Ref.	Debit	Credit	Balance	
						Debit	Credit
9/1	XX	Balance forward	√			8 5 00	

PHONE EXPENSE   ACCOUNT NO. 5040

Date		Explanation	Post Ref.	Debit	Credit	Balance	
						Debit	Credit
9/1	XX	Balance forward	√			1 5 5 00	

SUPPLIES EXPENSE   ACCOUNT NO. 5050

Date		Explanation	Post Ref.	Debit	Credit	Balance	
						Debit	Credit

INSURANCE EXPENSE   ACCOUNT NO. 5060

Date		Explanation	Post Ref.	Debit	Credit	Balance	
						Debit	Credit
9/1	XX	Balance forward	√			1 5 0 00	

POSTAGE EXPENSE   ACCOUNT NO. 5070

Date		Explanation	Post Ref.	Debit	Credit	Balance	
						Debit	Credit
9/1	XX	Balance forward	√			5 0 00	

ELDORADO COMPUTER CENTER
TRIAL BALANCE
SEPTEMBER 30, 19XX

	Dr.	Cr.

ELDORADO COMPUTER CENTER
INCOME STATEMENT
FOR THE QUARTER ENDED 9/30/XX

ELDORADO COMPUTER CENTER
STATEMENT OF OWNER'S EQUITY
FOR THE QUARTER ENDED 9/30/XX

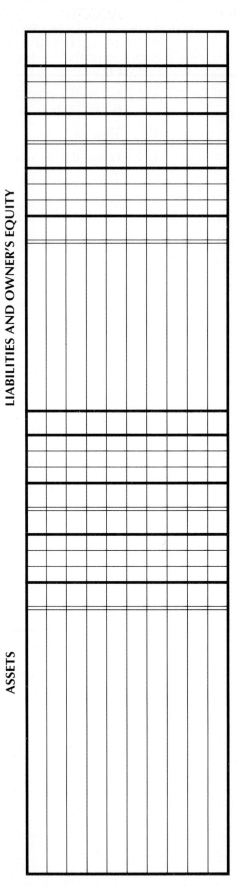

SOLUTIONS TO ACCOUNTING RECALL

Part I

1.	H	**6.**	D
2.	J	**7.**	A
3.	G	**8.**	I
4.	F	**9.**	E
5.	B	**10.**	C

Part II

11. False; (Different Books)

12. True

13. False; (Before or After Posting)

14. True

15. True

ACCOUNTING CYCLE CONTINUED: PREPARING WORKSHEETS AND FINANCIAL REPORTS

4

SELF-REVIEW QUIZ 4-1

Use a blank fold-out worksheet located in envelope at the end of this study guide.

SELF-REVIEW QUIZ 4-2

(1) _____

(2) _____

LIABILITIES AND OWNER'S EQUITY

ASSETS

(3)

FORMS FOR COMPREHENSIVE DEMONSTRATION PROBLEM

(1)
Use a blank fold-out worksheet located at the end of this study guide.

(2)

FROST COMPANY
INCOME STATEMENT
FOR MONTH ENDED DECEMBER 31, 19XX

(2)

FROST COMPANY
STATEMENT OF OWNER'S EQUITY
FOR MONTH ENDED DECEMBER 31, 19XX

COMPREHENSIVE DEMONSTRATION PROBLEM (CONCLUDED)

(2)

FROST COMPANY
BALANCE SHEET
DECEMBER 31, 19XX

ASSETS

LIABILITIES AND OWNER'S EQUITY

YOU MAKE THE CALL: CRITICAL THINKING/ETHICAL CASE

CHAPTER 4
FORMS FOR MINI EXERCISES

1. A.
    _____
    _____
    _____
    _____

    B.

1 Accounts Affected	2. Category	↑ 3 ↓	4 Rules	5 T-Account

    C.
    _____
    _____
    _____

2. A.
    _____
    _____
    _____
    _____

    B.

1 Accounts Affected	2. Category	↑ 3 ↓	4 Rules	5 T-Account

    C.
    _____
    _____

3. A. _____
    B. _____
    C.

1 Accounts Affected	2. Category	↑ 3 ↓	4 Rules	5 T-Account

    D.
    _____
    _____
    _____

4. A.

1 Accounts Affected	2. Category	↑ 3 ↓	4 Rules	5 T-Account

B.
_____
_____
_____

5.

A. _____	H. _____
B. _____	I. _____
C. _____	J. _____
D. _____	K. _____
E. _____	L. _____
F. _____	M. _____
G. _____	N. _____

6.

_____
_____
_____
_____
_____
_____
_____
_____

Name_____ Class _____ Date _____

FORMS FOR EXERCISES

4-1.

Account	Category	Normal Balance	Financial Report(s) Found on

4-2.

Accounts Affected	Category	Rules	Amount
A.			
B.			

4-3.

A. _____

B. _____
   _____
   _____

4-4.

Use a blank fold-out worksheet located at the end of this study guide.

EXERCISES (CONTINUED)

4-5.

(A)

J. TRENT
INCOME STATEMENT
FOR MONTH ENDED DECEMBER 31, 19XX

(B)

J. TRENT
STATEMENT OF OWNER'S EQUITY
FOR MONTH ENDED DECEMBER 31, 19XX

EXERCISES (CONTINUED)

(C)

J. TRENT
BALANCE SHEET
DECEMBER 31, 19XX

ASSETS

LIABILITIES AND OWNER'S EQUITY

END OF CHAPTER PROBLEMS

PROBLEM 4A-1 OR PROBLEM 4B-1

Use a blank fold-out worksheet located at the end of this study guide.

PROBLEM 4A-2 OR PROBLEM 4B-2

Use a blank fold-out worksheet located at the end of this study guide.

PROBLEM 4A-3 OR PROBLEM 4B-3

Use a blank fold-out worksheet located at the end of this study guide.

(2)

KEVIN'S MOVING CO.
INCOME STATEMENT
FOR MONTH ENDED OCTOBER 31, 19XX

KEVIN'S MOVING CO.
STATEMENT OF OWNER'S EQUITY
FOR MONTH ENDED OCTOBER 31, 19XX

(2)

PROBLEM 4A-3 OR PROBLEM 4B-3

(2)

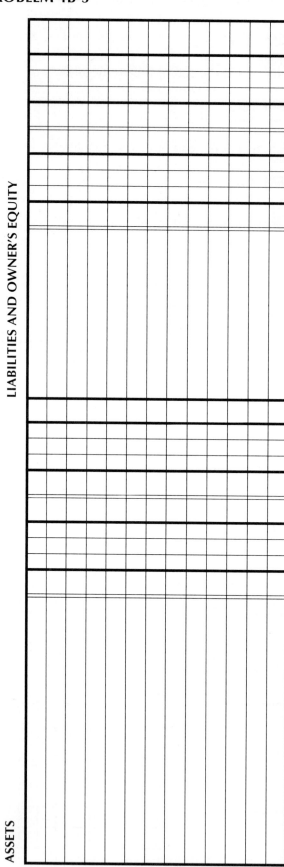

KEVIN'S MOVING CO.
BALANCE SHEET
OCTOBER 31, 19XX

LIABILITIES AND OWNER'S EQUITY

ASSETS

PROBLEM 4A-4 OR PROBLEM 4B-4

Use a blank fold-out worksheet located at the end of this study guide.

(2)

DICK'S REPAIR SERVICE
INCOME STATEMENT
FOR MONTH ENDED NOVEMBER 30, 19XX

(2)

DICK'S REPAIR SERVICE
STATEMENT OF OWNER'S EQUITY
FOR MONTH ENDED NOVEMBER 30, 19XX

PROBLEM 4A-4 OR PROBLEM 4B-4 (CONCLUDED)
(2)

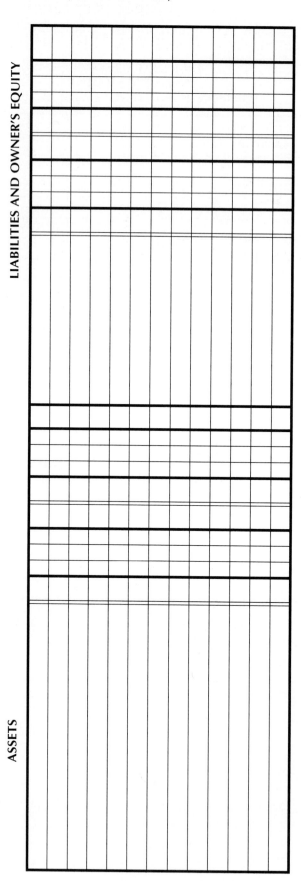

DICK'S REPAIR SERVICE
BALANCE SHEET
NOVEMBER 30, 19XX

LIABILITIES AND OWNER'S EQUITY

ASSETS

CHAPTER 4
SUMMARY PRACTICE TEST:
THE ACCOUNTING CYCLE CONTINUED:
PREPARING WORKSHEETS AND FINANCIAL REPORTS

Part I Instructions

Fill in the blank(s) to complete the statement.

1. Adjustments are the result of _____ transactions.
2. A _____ will increase acculumated depreciation.
3. _____ affect both the income statement and balance sheet.
4. The adjustment for supplies reflects the amount of supplies _____
   _____.
5. Supplies Expense is found on the income statement. Supplies are found on a
   _____ _____.
6. _____ _____ reflects the amount of equipment at
   time of purchase.
7. Depreciation Expense is found on the _____ _____.
8. _____ _____ is a contra asset that has a credit
   balance.
9. Accumulated Depreciation, a contra asset, is found on the _____
   _____.
10. Historical or original cost of an auto less _____
    _____ reflects the unused amount of the auto on the accounting books.
11. Withdrawals are found in the _____ column of the balance sheet
    section of the worksheet.
12. Salaries Payable is a liability that will appear in the _____
    _____ _____ _____ of the
    worksheet.
13. The figure for net income on the worksheet is carried over to the _____
    column of the balance sheet.
14. A worksheet is a(n)_____ report.
15. _____ _____ are prepared after the
    completion of the worksheet.

Part II Instructions

Complete the following statements by circling the letter of the appropriate answer.

1. Adjustments will affect
   a. the balance sheet
   b. the income statement
   c. both a and b

2. The historical or original cost of an asset on the worksheet
   a. never changes
   b. sometimes changes
   c. continually changes

3. Net income on the worksheet is
   a. carried over to the trial balance
   b. carried over to the adjusted trial balance
   c. carried over to the balance sheet column

4. Accumulated Depreciation is found on
   a. a worksheet
   b. an income statement
   c. both a worksheet and an income statement

5. Accumulated Depreciation, a contra asset, is increased by a
   a. debit
   b. credit
   c. both a and b

6. A worksheet is usually competed
   a. one column at a time
   b. two columns at a time
   c. three columns at a time

7. Withdrawals on the worksheet are found in the
   a. debit column of the income statement
   b. debit column of the balance sheet
   c. both a and b

8. The worksheet specifically shows the
   a. beginning figure for owner capital
   b. ending figure for owner capital
   c. average figure for owner capital

9. The total of the assets on a formal balance sheet will _____ equal the total of the debit column of the balance sheet on the worksheet.
   a. always
   b. sometimes
   c. never

10. The adjustment for depreciation affects
    a. the income statement
    b. the balance sheet
    c. both a and b

11. The adjustment for supplies requires one to know
    a. beginning supplies plus supplies purchased
    b. supplies on hand
    c. both a and b

12. The purpose of adjustments is to
>   a. bring general journals up to date
>   b. bring ledger accounts up to proper balances in the journal
>   c. bring ledger accounts to proper balance

13. Book values equals cost less
>   a. expenses
>   b. accumulated depreciation
>   c. neither a nor b

14. The _____ is an informal report.
>   a. income statement
>   b. balance sheet
>   c. worksheet

Part III Instructions

Answer true or false to the following statements.

1. The normal balance of accumulated depreciation is a debit.
2. Assets are only income statement accounts.
3. The total of the adjustments column may balance but be incorrect.
4. Prepaid rent is found on the income statement.
5. Rent expense is found on the income statement.
6. Debits and credits are found on formal reports.
7. Historical cost relates only to automobiles.
8. Accumulated Depreciation is found on the income statement.
9. As Accumulated Depreciation increases, the historical cost changes.
10. The adjustment for depreciation directly affects cash.
11. An expense is only recorded when it is paid.
12. The ending figure for owner capital does not have to be calculated from the worksheet.
13. Withdrawals have the same balance as Accumulated Depreciation.
14. Salaries Payable is an asset on the income statement.
15. Net loss would never be shown on a worksheet.
16. The net income on the worksheet is the same amount on the income statement.
17. Worksheets must use dollar signs.
18. The worksheet eliminates the need to prepare financial reports.
19. Cost less accumulated depreciation equals book value.
20. Accrued Salaries are expenses that have already been paid for.

CHAPTER 4
SOLUTIONS TO SUMMARY PRACTICE TEST

Part I

1. internal
2. credit
3. adjustments
4. used up
5. balance sheet
6. historical (original) cost
7. income statement
8. Accumulated Depreciation
9. balance sheet
10. Accumulated Depreciation
11. debit
12. balance sheet credit
13. credit
14. informal
15. financial statements

Part II

1. c
2. a
3. c
4. a
5. b
6. b
7. b
8. a
9. c
10. c
11. c
12. c
13. b
14. c

Part III

1. false
2. false
3. true
4. false
5. true
6. false
7. false
8. false
9. false
10. false
11. false
12. true
13. false
14. false
15. false
16. true
17. false
18. false
19. true
20. false

CHAPTERS 1-4
ACCOUNTING RECALL FORMS

Part I   **Part II**

1. ____   6. ____   11. _____

2. ____   7. ____   12. _____

3. ____   8. ____   13. _____

4. ____   9. ____   14. _____

5. ____   10. ____   15. _____

CONTINUING PROBLEM FOR CHAPTER 4*

ELDORADO COMPUTER CENTER
INCOME STATEMENT
FOR THE THREE MONTHS ENDED 9/30/XX

ELDORADO COMPUTER CENTER
STATEMENT OF OWNER'S EQUITY
FOR THE THREE MONTHS ENDED SEPTEMBER 30, 19XX

*Use a blank fold-out worksheet located at the end of this study guide.

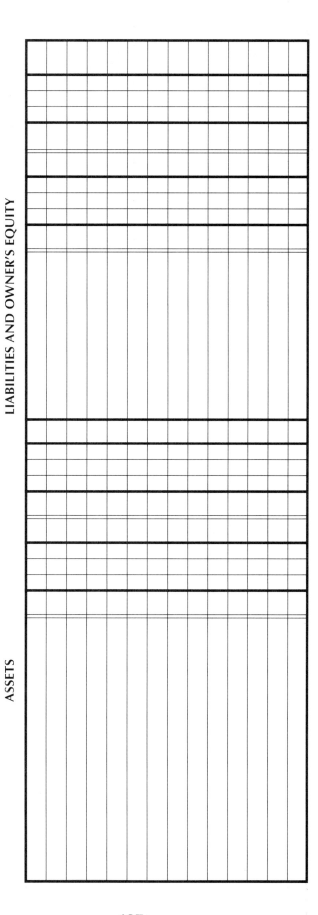

ELDORADO COMPUTER CENTER
BALANCE SHEET
SEPTEMBER 30, 19XX

ASSETS

LIABILITIES AND OWNER'S EQUITY

SOLUTIONS TO ACCOUNTING RECALL

Part I

1.	E	**6.**	A
2.	B	**7.**	G
3.	H	**8.**	D
4.	J	**9.**	F
5.	I	**10.**	C

Part II

11. False; (Internal Transaction)

12. False; (Both Income Statements as Balance Sheet)

13. True

14. False; (Credit)

15. True

THE ACCOUNTING CYCLE COMPLETED: ADJUSTING, CLOSING, AND THE POST-CLOSING TRIAL BALANCE

5

SELF-REVIEW QUIZ 5-1

(1)

PAGE 2

Date	Account Titles and Description	PR	Dr.	Cr.

(2) Partial Ledger

| Depreciation Expense, Store Equipment | 511 | | Accumulated Depreciation, Store Equipment | 122 |

| | | | 4 | |

| Prepaid Insurance | 116 | | Insurance Expense | 516 |

| 3 | | | | |

| Store Supplies | 114 | | Supplies Expense | 514 |

| 5 | | | | |

| Salaries Expense | 512 | | Salaries Payable | 212 |

| 8 | | | | |

SELF-REVIEW QUIZ 5-2

P. Logan, Capital 310	Revenue from Clients 410	Supplies Expense 514
14	25	4

P. Logan, Withdrawals 311	Depreciation Expense, Store Equipment 510	Insurance Expense 516
3	1	2

Income Summary 312	Salaries Expense 512	Rent Expense 518
	11	2

(2) _____

_____

_____

_____

SELF-REVIEW QUIZ 5-3

_____

_____

_____

FORMS FOR COMPREHENSIVE DEMONSTRATION PROBLEM

(Worksheet is a fold-out at end of study guide/working paper)

ROLO COMPANY
GENERAL JOURNAL

PAGE 1

Date	Account Titles and Description	PR	Dr.	Cr.

FORMS FOR COMPREHENSIVE DEMONSTRATION PROBLEM (CONTINUED)

ROLO COMPANY
GENERAL JOURNAL

Date	Account Titles and Description	PR	Dr.	Cr.

FORMS FOR COMPREHENSIVE DEMONSTRATION PROBLEM (CONTINUED)

CASH   ACCOUNT NO. 111

Date	Explanation	Post Ref.	Debit	Credit	Balance Debit	Balance Credit

ACCOUNTS RECEIVABLE   ACCOUNT NO. 112

Date	Explanation	Post Ref.	Debit	Credit	Balance Debit	Balance Credit

PREPAID RENT   ACCOUNT NO. 114

Date	Explanation	Post Ref.	Debit	Credit	Balance Debit	Balance Credit

OFFICE SUPPLIES   ACCOUNT NO. 115

Date	Explanation	Post Ref.	Debit	Credit	Balance Debit	Balance Credit

FORMS FOR COMPREHENSIVE DEMONSTRATION PROBLEM (CONTINUED)

OFFICE EQUIPMENT   ACCOUNT NO. 121

Date	Explanation	Post Ref.	Debit	Credit	Balance Debit	Balance Credit

ACCUMULATED DEPRECIATION, OFFICE EQUIPMENT   ACCOUNT NO. 122

Date	Explanation	Post Ref.	Debit	Credit	Balance Debit	Balance Credit

ACCOUNTS PAYABLE   ACCOUNT NO. 211

Date	Explanation	Post Ref.	Debit	Credit	Balance Debit	Balance Credit

Name _____ Class _____ Date _____

FORMS FOR COMPREHENSIVE DEMONSTRATION PROBLEM (CONTINUED)

SALARIES PAYABLE   ACCOUNT NO. 212

Date	Explanation	Post Ref.	Debit	Credit	Balance Debit	Balance Credit

ROLO KERN, CAPITAL   ACCOUNT NO. 311

Date	Explanation	Post Ref.	Debit	Credit	Balance Debit	Balance Credit

ROLO KERN, WITHDRAWALS   ACCOUNT NO. 312

Date	Explanation	Post Ref.	Debit	Credit	Balance Debit	Balance Credit

INCOME SUMMARY   ACCOUNT NO. 313

Date	Explanation	Post Ref.	Debit	Credit	Balance Debit	Balance Credit

FEES EARNED   ACCOUNT NO. 411

Date	Explanation	Post Ref.	Debit	Credit	Balance Debit	Balance Credit

FORMS FOR COMPREHENSIVE DEMONSTRATION PROBLEM (CONTINUED)

SALARIES EXPENSE   ACCOUNT NO. 511

Date	Explanation	Post Ref.	Debit	Credit	Balance Debit	Balance Credit

ADVERTISING EXPENSE   ACCOUNT NO. 512

Date	Explanation	Post Ref.	Debit	Credit	Balance Debit	Balance Credit

RENT EXPENSE   ACCOUNT NO. 513

Date	Explanation	Post Ref.	Debit	Credit	Balance Debit	Balance Credit

OFFICE SUPPLIES EXPENSE   ACCOUNT NO. 514

Date	Explanation	Post Ref.	Debit	Credit	Balance Debit	Balance Credit

DEPRECIATION EXPENSE, OFFICE EQUIPMENT   ACCOUNT NO. 515

Date	Explanation	Post Ref.	Debit	Credit	Balance Debit	Balance Credit

FORMS FOR COMPREHENSIVE DEMONSTRATION PROBLEM (CONTINUED)

ROLO COMPANY
INCOME STATEMENT
FOR MONTH ENDED JANUARY 31, 19XX

ROLO COMPANY
STATEMENT OF OWNER'S EQUITY
FOR MONTH ENDED JANUARY 31, 19XX

FORMS FOR COMPREHENSIVE DEMONSTRATION PROBLEM (CONTINUED)

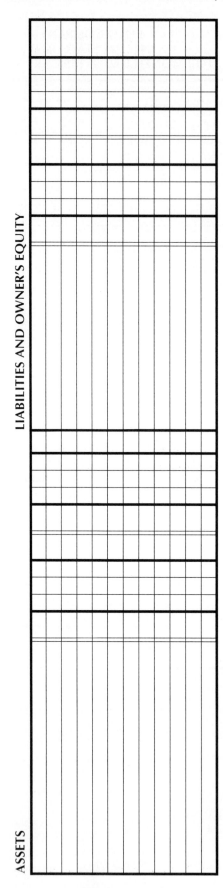

ROLO COMPANY
BALANCE SHEET
JANUARY 31, 19XX

LIABILITIES AND OWNER'S EQUITY

ASSETS

FORMS FOR COMPREHENSIVE DEMONSTRATION PROBLEM (CONCLUDED)

ROLO COMPANY
POST-CLOSING TRIAL BALANCE
JANUARY 31, 19XX

	Dr.	Cr.

YOU MAKE THE CALL: CRITICAL THINKING/ETHICAL CASE

_____
_____
_____
_____
_____
_____
_____
_____
_____
_____
_____
_____
_____
_____
_____
_____
_____
_____
_____
_____
_____
_____
_____
_____
_____
_____
_____
_____
_____
_____
_____
_____
_____
_____
_____
_____
_____
_____
_____

Name Lauren Peterson   Class Accounting   Date Dec. 8, 1998

CHAPTER 5
FORMS FOR MINI EXERCISES
GENERAL JOURNAL

1.

Date		Account Titles and Description	PR		Dr.				Cr.		
Dec.	31	Insurance Expense				6	00				
		Prepaid Insurance								6	00
	31	Supplies Expense				3	00				
		Store Supplies								3	00
	31	Depr. Exp., Store Equip.				7	00				
		Accum. Depr., Store Equip								7	00
	31	Salaries Expense				4	00				
		Salaries Payable								4	00

2. _____
_____
_____
_____
_____
_____
_____
_____
_____

143

3.

4.

Income Summary   314

_____

5.

Mel Blanc, Capital   310

_____

FORMS FOR EXERCISES

5-1.

Date		Account Titles and Description	PR		Dr.			Cr.	

5-2.

	TEMPORARY	PERMANENT	WILL BE CLOSED
1. Income Summary			
2. A. Rose, Capital			
3. Salary Expense			
4. A. Rose, Withdrawals			
5. Fees Earned			
6. Accounts Payable			
7. Cash			

5-3.

Date		Account Titles and Description	PR		Dr.					Cr.			

EXERCISES (CONTINUED)

5-4.

Date	Account Titles and Description	PR	Dr.	Cr.

5-5.

WEY CO.
POST-CLOSING TRIAL BALANCE
DECEMBER 31, 19XX

	Dr.	Cr.

PROBLEM 5A-1 OR PROBLEM 5B-1

Use a blank fold-out worksheet located at the end of this study guide.
(2)

MARC'S CONSULTING SERVICE
GENERAL JOURNAL

PAGE 3

Date	Account Titles and Description	PR	Dr.	Cr.

PROBLEM 5A-2 OR PROBLEM 5B-2

(1)

POTTER CLEANING SERVICE
GENERAL JOURNAL

Date		Account Titles and Description	PR	Dr.		Cr.	

PROBLEM 5A-2 OR PROBLEM 5B-2 (CONTINUED)

CASH   ACCOUNT NO. 112

Date	Explanation	Post Ref.	Debit	Credit	Balance Debit	Balance Credit

PREPAID INSURANCE   ACCOUNT NO. 114

Date	Explanation	Post Ref.	Debit	Credit	Balance Debit	Balance Credit

CLEANING SUPPLIES   ACCOUNT NO. 115

Date	Explanation	Post Ref.	Debit	Credit	Balance Debit	Balance Credit

AUTO   ACCOUNT NO. 121

Date	Explanation	Post Ref.	Debit	Credit	Balance Debit	Balance Credit

ACCUMULATED DEPRECIATION, AUTO   ACCOUNT NO. 122

Date	Explanation	Post Ref.	Debit	Credit	Balance Debit	Balance Credit

PROBLEM 5A-2 OR PROBLEM 5B-2 (CONTINUED)

ACCOUNTS PAYABLE ACCOUNT NO. 212

Date	Explanation	Post Ref.	Debit	Credit	Balance Debit	Balance Credit

SALARIES PAYABLE ACCOUNT NO. 213

Date	Explanation	Post Ref.	Debit	Credit	Balance Debit	Balance Credit

B. POTTER, CAPITAL ACCOUNT NO. 312

Date	Explanation	Post Ref.	Debit	Credit	Balance Debit	Balance Credit

B. POTTER, WITHDRAWALS ACCOUNT NO. 313

Date	Explanation	Post Ref.	Debit	Credit	Balance Debit	Balance Credit

INCOME SUMMARY ACCOUNT NO. 314

Date	Explanation	Post Ref.	Debit	Credit	Balance Debit	Balance Credit

PROBLEM 5A-2 OR PROBLEM 5B-2 (CONTINUED)

CLEANING FEES   **ACCOUNT NO. 412**

Date	Explanation	Post Ref.	Debit	Credit	Balance Debit	Balance Credit

SALARIES EXPENSE   **ACCOUNT NO. 513**

Date	Explanation	Post Ref.	Debit	Credit	Balance Debit	Balance Credit

TELEPHONE EXPENSE   **ACCOUNT NO. 514**

Date	Explanation	Post Ref.	Debit	Credit	Balance Debit	Balance Credit

ADVERTISING EXPENSE   **ACCOUNT NO. 515**

Date	Explanation	Post Ref.	Debit	Credit	Balance Debit	Balance Credit

GAS EXPENSE   **ACCOUNT NO. 516**

Date	Explanation	Post Ref.	Debit	Credit	Balance Debit	Balance Credit

PROBLEM 5A-2 OR PROBLEM 5B-2 (CONTINUED)

INSURANCE EXPENSE ACCOUNT NO. 517

Date	Explanation	Post Ref.	Debit	Credit	Balance Debit	Balance Credit

CLEANING SUPPLIES EXPENSE ACCOUNT NO. 518

Date	Explanation	Post Ref.	Debit	Credit	Balance Debit	Balance Credit

DEPRECIATION EXPENSE, AUTO ACCOUNT NO. 519

Date	Explanation	Post Ref.	Debit	Credit	Balance Debit	Balance Credit

PROBLEM 5A-2 OR PROBLEM 5B-2 (CONCLUDED)

POTTER CLEANING SERVICE
POST-CLOSING TRIAL BALANCE
MARCH 31, 19XX

			Dr.			Cr.	

PROBLEM 5A-3 OR PROBLEM 5B-3

Use a blank fold-out worksheet located at the end of this study guide.

PROBLEM 5A-3 OR PROBLEM 5B-3 (CONTINUED)

PETE'S PLOWING
GENERAL JOURNAL

PAGE 1

Date	Account Titles and Description	PR	Dr.	Cr.

PROBLEM 5A-3 OR PROBLEM 5B-3 (CONTINUED)

PETE'S PLOWING
GENERAL JOURNAL

PAGE 2

Date		Account Titles and Description	PR		Dr.			Cr.	

PROBLEM 5A-3 OR PROBLEM 5B-3 (CONTINUED)

PETE'S PLOWING
GENERAL JOURNAL

PAGE 3

Date		Account Titles and Description	PR		Dr.		Cr.	

PROBLEM 5A-3 OR PROBLEM 5B-3 (CONTINUED)

CASH   ACCOUNT NO. 111

Date	Explanation	Post Ref.	Debit	Credit	Balance	
					Debit	Credit

ACCOUNTS RECEIVABLE   ACCOUNT NO. 112

Date	Explanation	Post Ref.	Debit	Credit	Balance	
					Debit	Credit

PREPAID RENT   ACCOUNT NO. 114

Date	Explanation	Post Ref.	Debit	Credit	Balance	
					Debit	Credit

SNOW SUPPLIES   ACCOUNT NO. 115

Date	Explanation	Post Ref.	Debit	Credit	Balance	
					Debit	Credit

PROBLEM 5A-3 OR PROBLEM 5B-3 (CONTINUED)

OFFICE EQUIPMENT   ACCOUNT NO. 121

Date	Explanation	Post Ref.	Debit	Credit	Balance	
					Debit	Credit

ACCUMULATED DEPRECIATION, OFFICE EQUIPMENT   ACCOUNT NO. 122

Date	Explanation	Post Ref.	Debit	Credit	Balance	
					Debit	Credit

SNOW EQUIPMENT   ACCOUNT NO. 123

Date	Explanation	Post Ref.	Debit	Credit	Balance	
					Debit	Credit

ACCUMULATED DEPRECIATION, SNOW EQUIPMENT   ACCOUNT NO. 124

Date	Explanation	Post Ref.	Debit	Credit	Balance	
					Debit	Credit

ACCOUNTS PAYABLE   ACCOUNT NO. 211

Date	Explanation	Post Ref.	Debit	Credit	Balance	
					Debit	Credit

PROBLEM 5A-3 OR PROBLEM 5B-3 (CONTINUED)

SALARIES PAYABLE   ACCOUNT NO. 212

Date	Explanation	Post Ref.	Debit	Credit	Balance Debit	Balance Credit

PETE MACK, CAPITAL   ACCOUNT NO. 311

Date	Explanation	Post Ref.	Debit	Credit	Balance Debit	Balance Credit

PETE MACK, WITHDRAWALS   ACCOUNT NO. 312

Date	Explanation	Post Ref.	Debit	Credit	Balance Debit	Balance Credit

INCOME SUMMARY   ACCOUNT NO. 313

Date	Explanation	Post Ref.	Debit	Credit	Balance Debit	Balance Credit

PLOWING FEES   ACCOUNT NO. 411

Date	Explanation	Post Ref.	Debit	Credit	Balance Debit	Balance Credit

PROBLEM 5A-3 OR PROBLEM 5B-3 (CONTINUED)

SALARIES EXPENSE   ACCOUNT NO. 511

Date	Explanation	Post Ref.	Debit	Credit	Balance Debit	Balance Credit

ADVERTISING EXPENSE   ACCOUNT NO. 512

Date	Explanation	Post Ref.	Debit	Credit	Balance Debit	Balance Credit

TELEPHONE EXPENSE   ACCOUNT NO. 513

Date	Explanation	Post Ref.	Debit	Credit	Balance Debit	Balance Credit

RENT EXPENSE   ACCOUNT NO. 514

Date	Explanation	Post Ref.	Debit	Credit	Balance Debit	Balance Credit

SNOW SUPPLIES EXPENSE   ACCOUNT NO. 515

Date	Explanation	Post Ref.	Debit	Credit	Balance Debit	Balance Credit

PROBLEM 5A-3 OR PROBLEM 5B-3 (CONTINUED)

DEPRECIATION EXPENSE, OFFICE EQUIPMENT   ACCOUNT NO. 516

Date	Explanation	Post Ref.	Debit	Credit	Balance	
					Debit	Credit

DEPRECIATION EXPENSE, SNOW EQUIPMENT   ACCOUNT NO. 517

Date	Explanation	Post Ref.	Debit	Credit	Balance	
					Debit	Credit

PROBLEM 5A-3 OR PROBLEM 5B-3 (CONTINUED)

PETE'S PLOWING
INCOME STATEMENT
FOR MONTH ENDED JANUARY 31, 19XX

PETE'S PLOWING
STATEMENT OF OWNER'S EQUITY
FOR MONTH ENDED JANUARY 31, 19XX

PROBLEM 5A-3 OR PROBLEM 5B-3 (CONTINUED)

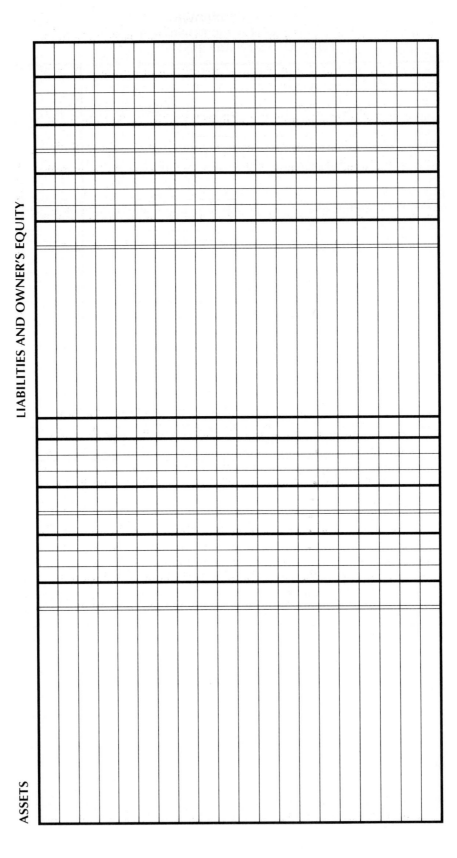

PETE'S PLOWING
BALANCE SHEET
JANUARY 31, 19XX

ASSETS

LIABILITIES AND OWNER'S EQUITY

PROBLEM 5A-3 OR PROBLEM 5B-3 (CONCLUDED)

PETE'S PLOWING
POST-CLOSING TRIAL BALANCE
JANUARY 31, 19XX

		Dr.		Cr.	

CHAPTER 5
SUMMARY PRACTICE TEST:
THE ACCOUNTING CYCLE COMPLETED:
ADJUSTING, CLOSING, AND
THE POST-CLOSING TRIAL BALANCE

Part I Instructions

Fill in the blank(s) to complete the statement.

1. Income summary is _____ by the end of the period.
2. Revenue, Expenses, and Withdrawals are examples of _____ _____.
3. _____ in temporary accounts will not be carried over to the next accounting period.
4. After closing entries are posted, owner's Capital in the ledger will contain the _____ _____.
5. Revenue is closed to Income Summary by a _____ to each revenue account and a _____ to Income Summary.
6. Expenses are closed to Income Summary by _____ the individual expenses and _____ Income Summary.
7. If the balance of Income Summary is a credit, it will be closed by _____ Income Summary and _____ owner's Capital.
8. The balance of Withdrawals is closed by a _____ and the amount transferred to owner's Capital by a _____.
9. At the end of the closing process, all temporary accounts in the ledger will have a _____ balance.
10. The _____ _____ _____ contains a list of permanent accounts after the adjusting and closing entries have been posted to the ledger from a journal.
11. Closing entries can be prepared from a _____ _____.
12. After closing entries are posted, Income Summary will have a _____ balance.
13. Journalizing adjustments can be done from the _____ _____.
14. Cash, Equipment, and Supplies are not part of the _____ process.
15. Income Summary is a _____ account.

Part II Instructions

The following is a chart of accounts for Jim's Fix-it Shop. From the chart, indicate in Column B (by account number) which accounts will be debited or credited as related to the transactions in Column A.

CHART OF ACCOUNTS

ASSETS	OWNER'S EQUITY
112 Cash	340 M. Delicious, Capital
114 Accounts Receivable	341 M. Delicious, Withdrawals
116 Prepaid Rent	342 Income Summary
118 Fix-It Supplies	
120 Truck	REVENUE
121 Accumulated Depreciation, Truck	450 Fix-It Fees Earned
LIABILITIES	EXPENSES
230 Accounts Payable	560 Salaries
232 Salaries Payable	562 Advertising
	564 Rent
	566 Fix-It Supplies
	568 Depreciation Expense, Truck

COLUMN A	COLUMN B	
	Debit(s)	Credit(s)
1. Closed balance in revenue account to Income Summary.	_____	_____
2. Closed balance in individual expenses to Income Summary	_____	_____
3 Closed balance in Income Summary to owner's Capital. (Assume that it is a net income.)	_____	_____
4. Closed Withdrawals to owner's Capital.	_____	_____
5. Recorded Fix-It supplies used up.	_____	_____
6. Recorded depreciation on truck.	_____	_____
7. Brought Salaries Expense up to date (an adjustment).	_____	_____

Part III Instructions

Answer true or false to the following statements.

1. All companies journalize and post closing entries before the end of their calendar year.
2. Adjustments are journalized before preparing the worksheet.
3. Closing entries can only clear permanent accounts.
4. Income summary is a temporary account.
5. Interim reports can be prepared from worksheets.
6. To clear expenses in the closing process, a compound entry is appropriate.
7. Withdrawals is a permanent account.
8. Income Summary helps update withdrawals.

9. Accumulated Depreciation is a temporary account.

10. Cash, Rent Expense, and Accounts Receivable need to be closed at the end of the period.

11. Closing entries do not relate to the worksheet.

12. Revenue is closed by a credit.

13. Expenses are placed on the debit side of the Income Summary account.

14. A post-closing trial balance closely resembles the ending balance sheet.

15. Accumulated Depreciation never has to be adjusted.

16. Interim reports are always prepared monthly.

17. A post-closing trial balance is prepared before adjustments are journalized.

18. Income Summary is shown on the balance sheet.

19. The process of closing entries will help update owner's Capital.

20. An increase in Income Summary is a debit.

21. An increase in Income Summary is a credit.

22. The income statement is listed in terms of debits and credits.

23. Closing updates only permanent accounts.

24. The completion of financial reports means that the Capital account in the ledger has been updated.

25. Withdrawals is closed to Income Summary.

SOLUTIONS TO SUMMARY PRACTICE TEST

Part I

1. closed
2. temporary accounts
3. balances
4. ending figure (balance)
5. debit, credit
6. crediting, debiting
7. debiting, crediting
8. credit, debit
9. zero
10. post-closing trial balance
11. worksheet
12. zero
13. worksheet
14. closing
15. temporary

Part II

	Debit	Credit
1.	450	342
2.	342	560, 562, 564, 566, 568
3.	342	340
4.	340	341
5.	566	118
6.	568	121
7.	560	232

Part III

1. false	**7.** false	**13.** true	**19.** true	**25.** false
2. false	**8.** false	**14.** true	**20.** false	
3. false	**9.** false	**15.** false	**21.** false	
4. true	**10.** false	**16.** false	**22.** false	
5. true	**11.** false	**17.** false	**23.** false	
6. true	**12.** false	**18.** false	**24.** false	

CHAPTERS 1-5
ACCOUNTING RECALL FORMS

Part I

Part II

1. _____   6. _____

2. _____   7. _____

3. _____   8. _____

4. _____   9. _____

5. _____   10. _____

11._____

12._____

13._____

14._____

15._____

CONTINUING PROBLEM FOR CHAPTER 5

ELDORADO COMPUTER CENTER
GENERAL JOURNAL

PAGE 2

Date	Account Titles and Description	PR	Dr.	Cr.

CASH   ACCOUNT NO. 1000

Date	Explanation	Post Ref.	Debit	Credit	Balance Debit	Balance Credit
9/30 XX	Balance forward	√			1 6 4 5 00	

ACCOUNTS RECEIVABLE   ACCOUNT NO. 1020

Date	Explanation	Post Ref.	Debit	Credit	Balance Debit	Balance Credit
9/30 XX	Balance forward	√			2 6 0 0 00	

PREPAID RENT   ACCOUNT NO. 1025

Date	Explanation	Post Ref.	Debit	Credit	Balance Debit	Balance Credit
9/30 XX	Balance forward	√			1 2 0 0 00	

SUPPLIES   ACCOUNT NO. 1030

Date	Explanation	Post Ref.	Debit	Credit	Balance Debit	Balance Credit
9/30 XX	Balance forward	√			4 5 0 00	

COMPUTER SHOP EQUIPMENT   ACCOUNT NO. 1080

Date		Explanation	Post Ref.	Debit	Credit	Balance Debit	Balance Credit
9/30	XX	Balance forward	√			2 4 0 0 00	

ACCUMULATED DEPRECIATION, COMPUTER SHOP EQUIPMENT ACCOUNT NO. 1081

Date		Explanation	Post Ref.	Debit	Credit	Balance Debit	Balance Credit

OFFICE EQUIPMENT   ACCOUNT NO. 1090

Date		Explanation	Post Ref.	Debit	Credit	Balance Debit	Balance Credit
9/30	XX	Balance forward	√			6 0 0 00	

ACCUMULATED DEPRECIATION, OFFICE EQUIPMENT   ACCOUNT NO. 1091

Date		Explanation	Post Ref.	Debit	Credit	Balance Debit	Balance Credit

ACCOUNTS PAYABLE   ACCOUNT NO. 2000

Date	Explanation	Post Ref.	Debit	Credit	Balance Debit	Balance Credit
9/30 XX	Balance forward	√				2 1 0 00

T. FREEDMAN, CAPITAL   ACCOUNT NO. 3000

Date	Explanation	Post Ref.	Debit	Credit	Balance Debit	Balance Credit
9/30 XX	Balance forward	√				4 5 0 0 00

T. FREEDMAN, WITHDRAWALS   ACCOUNT NO. 3010

Date	Explanation	Post Ref.	Debit	Credit	Balance Debit	Balance Credit
9/30 XX	Balance forward	√			1 0 0 00	

INCOME SUMMARY   ACCOUNT NO. 3020

Date	Explanation	Post Ref.	Debit	Credit	Balance Debit	Balance Credit

SERVICE REVENUE   ACCOUNT NO. 4000

Date		Explanation	Post Ref.	Debit	Credit	Balance Debit	Balance Credit
9/30	XX	Balance forward	√				6 6 8 5 00

ADVERTISING EXPENSE   ACCOUNT NO. 5010

Date		Explanation	Post Ref.	Debit	Credit	Balance Debit	Balance Credit
9/30	XX	Balance forward	√			1 4 0 0 00	

RENT EXPENSE   ACCOUNT NO. 5020

Date		Explanation	Post Ref.	Debit	Credit	Balance Debit	Balance Credit
9/30	XX	Balance forward	√			4 0 0 00	

UTILITIES EXPENSE   ACCOUNT NO. <u>5030</u>

Date		Explanation	Post Ref.	Debit	Credit	Balance	
						Debit	Credit
9/30	XX	Balance forward	√			1 8 0 00	

PHONE EXPENSE   ACCOUNT NO. <u>5040</u>

Date		Explanation	Post Ref.	Debit	Credit	Balance	
						Debit	Credit
9/30	XX	Balance forward	√			2 2 0 00	

SUPPLIES EXPENSE   ACCOUNT NO. <u>5050</u>

Date		Explanation	Post Ref.	Debit	Credit	Balance	
						Debit	Credit

INSURANCE EXPENSE   ACCOUNT NO. <u>5060</u>

Date		Explanation	Post Ref.	Debit	Credit	Balance	
						Debit	Credit
9/30	XX	Balance forward	√			1 5 0 00	

POSTAGE EXPENSE   ACCOUNT NO. 5070

Date		Explanation	Post Ref.	Debit	Credit	Balance Debit	Balance Credit
9/30	XX	Balance forward	√			5 0 00	

DEPRECIATION EXPENSE C.S. EQUIPMENT   ACCOUNT NO. 5080

Date		Explanation	Post Ref.	Debit	Credit	Balance Debit	Balance Credit

DEPRECIATION EXPENSE OFFICE EQUIPMENT   ACCOUNT NO. 5090

Date		Explanation	Post Ref.	Debit	Credit	Balance Debit	Balance Credit

ELDORADO COMPUTER CENTER
POST-CLOSING TRIAL BALANCE
SEPTEMBER 30, 19XX

		Dr.		Cr.	

SOLUTIONS TO ACCOUNTING RECALL

Part I

1.	E		**6.**	F
2.	H		**7.**	D
3.	G		**8.**	A
4.	J		**9.**	I
5.	C		**10.**	B

Part II

11. False; Not a debit or credit

12. True

13. False; Can be done from a worksheet

14. True

15. False; Before

MINI PRACTICE SET
VALDEZ REALTY

VALDEZ REALTY
GENERAL JOURNAL

PAGE 1

Date	Account Titles and Description	PR	Dr.	Cr.

**MINI PRACTICE SET
VALDEZ REALTY**

**VALDEZ REALTY
GENERAL JOURNAL**

Date		Account Titles and Description	PR	Dr.	Cr.

MINI PRACTICE SET
VALDEZ REALTY

VALDEZ REALTY
GENERAL JOURNAL

PAGE 3

Date		Account Titles and Description	PR		Dr.				Cr.		

MINI PRACTICE SET
VALDEZ REALTY

VALDEZ REALTY
GENERAL JOURNAL

Date	Account Titles and Description	PR	Dr.	Cr.

MINI PRACTICE SET
VALDEZ REALTY

VALDEZ REALTY
GENERAL JOURNAL

PAGE 5

Date	Account Titles and Description	PR	Dr.	Cr.

MINI PRACTICE SET
VALDEZ REALTY

VALDEZ REALTY
GENERAL JOURNAL

Date	Account Titles and Description	PR	Dr.	Cr.

MINI PRACTICE SET
VALDEZ REALTY

CASH   **ACCOUNT NO. 111**

Date	Explanation	Post Ref.	Debit	Credit	Balance Debit	Balance Credit

MINI PRACTICE SET
VALDEZ REALTY

ACCOUNTS RECEIVABLE ACCOUNT NO. 112

Date	Explanation	Post Ref.	Debit	Credit	Balance Debit	Balance Credit

PREPAID RENT ACCOUNT NO. 114

Date	Explanation	Post Ref.	Debit	Credit	Balance Debit	Balance Credit

OFFICE SUPPLIES ACCOUNT NO. 115

Date	Explanation	Post Ref.	Debit	Credit	Balance Debit	Balance Credit

OFFICE EQUIPMENT ACCOUNT NO. 121

Date	Explanation	Post Ref.	Debit	Credit	Balance Debit	Balance Credit

MINI PRACTICE SET: VALDEZ REALTY

ACCUMULATED DEPRECIATION, OFFICE EQUIPMENT — ACCOUNT NO. 122

Date	Explanation	Post Ref.	Debit	Credit	Balance Debit	Balance Credit

AUTOMOBILE — ACCOUNT NO. 123

Date	Explanation	Post Ref.	Debit	Credit	Balance Debit	Balance Credit

ACCUMULATED DEPRECIATION, AUTOMOBILE — ACCOUNT NO. 124

Date	Explanation	Post Ref.	Debit	Credit	Balance Debit	Balance Credit

ACCOUNTS PAYABLE — ACCOUNT NO. 211

Date	Explanation	Post Ref.	Debit	Credit	Balance Debit	Balance Credit

SALARIES PAYABLE — ACCOUNT NO. 212

Date	Explanation	Post Ref.	Debit	Credit	Balance Debit	Balance Credit

MINI PRACTICE SET
VALDEZ REALTY

JUAN VALDEZ, CAPITAL   ACCOUNT NO. 311

Date	Explanation	Post Ref.	Debit	Credit	Balance Debit	Balance Credit

JUAN VALDEZ, WITHDRAWALS   ACCOUNT NO. 312

Date	Explanation	Post Ref.	Debit	Credit	Balance Debit	Balance Credit

INCOME SUMMARY   ACCOUNT NO. 313

Date	Explanation	Post Ref.	Debit	Credit	Balance Debit	Balance Credit

MINI PRACTICE SET
VALDEZ REALTY

COMMISSIONS EARNED   ACCOUNT NO. 411

Date	Explanation	Post Ref.	Debit	Credit	Balance Debit	Balance Credit

RENT EXPENSE   ACCOUNT NO. 511

Date	Explanation	Post Ref.	Debit	Credit	Balance Debit	Balance Credit

SALARIES EXPENSE   ACCOUNT NO. 512

Date	Explanation	Post Ref.	Debit	Credit	Balance Debit	Balance Credit

MINI PRACTICE SET
VALDEZ REALTY

GAS EXPENSE   ACCOUNT NO. 513

Date	Explanation	Post Ref.	Debit	Credit	Balance Debit	Balance Credit

REPAIRS EXPENSE   ACCOUNT NO. 514

Date	Explanation	Post Ref.	Debit	Credit	Balance Debit	Balance Credit

TELEPHONE EXPENSE   ACCOUNT NO. 515

Date	Explanation	Post Ref.	Debit	Credit	Balance Debit	Balance Credit

ADVERTISING EXPENSE   ACCOUNT NO. 516

Date	Explanation	Post Ref.	Debit	Credit	Balance Debit	Balance Credit

MINI PRACTICE SET
VALDEZ REALTY

OFFICE SUPPLIES EXPENSE   ACCOUNT NO. 517

Date	Explanation	Post Ref.	Debit	Credit	Balance Debit	Balance Credit

DEPRECIATION EXPENSE, OFFICE EQUIPMENT   ACCOUNT NO. 518

Date	Explanation	Post Ref.	Debit	Credit	Balance Debit	Balance Credit

DEPRECIATION EXPENSE, AUTOMOBILE   ACCOUNT NO. 519

Date	Explanation	Post Ref.	Debit	Credit	Balance Debit	Balance Credit

MISCELLANEOUS EXPENSE   ACCOUNT NO. 524

Date	Explanation	Post Ref.	Debit	Credit	Balance Debit	Balance Credit

MINI PRACTICE SET
VALDEZ REALTY

VALDEZ REALTY
INCOME STATEMENT
FOR MONTH ENDED JUNE 30, 19XX

COMPREHENSIVE REVIEW PROBLEM:
VALDEZ REALTY

Use blank fold-out worksheets located at the end of this study guide.

**MINI PRACTICE SET
VALDEZ REALTY**

**VALDEZ REALTY
STATEMENT OF OWNER'S EQUITY
FOR MONTH ENDED JUNE 30, 19XX**

MINI PRACTICE SET
VALDEZ REALTY

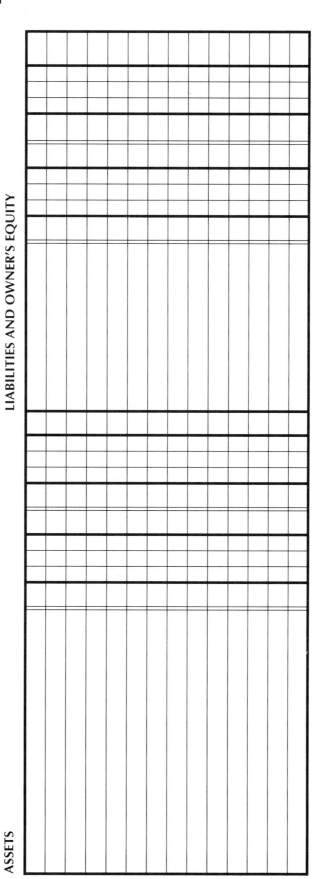

VALDEZ REALTY
BALANCE SHEET
JUNE 30, 19XX

LIABILITIES AND OWNER'S EQUITY

ASSETS

MINI PRACTICE SET
VALDEZ REALTY

VALDEZ REALTY
POST-CLOSING TRIAL BALANCE
JUNE 30, 19XX

	Dr.	Cr.

MINI PRACTICE SET
VALDEZ REALTY

VALDEZ REALTY
INCOME STATEMENT
FOR MONTH ENDED JULY 31, 19XX

MINI PRACTICE SET
VALDEZ REALTY

VALDEZ REALTY
STATEMENT OF OWNER'S EQUITY
FOR MONTH ENDED JULY 31, 19XX

MINI PRACTICE SET
VALDEZ REALTY

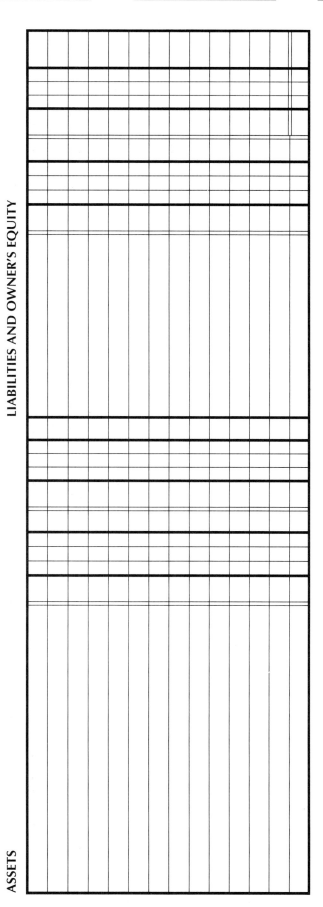

VALDEZ REALTY
BALANCE SHEET
JULY 31, 19XX

ASSETS

LIABILITIES AND OWNER'S EQUITY

MINI PRACTICE SET
VALDEZ REALTY

VALDEZ REALTY
POST-CLOSING TRIAL BALANCE
JULY 31, 19XX

		Dr.	Cr.

BANKING PROCEDURES AND CONTROL OF CASH

6

SELF-REVIEW QUIZ 6-1

Situation	Add to Bank Balance	Deduct from Bank Balance	Add to Checkbook Balance	Deduct from Checkbook Balance
1				
2				
3				
4				
5				
6				

SELF-REVIEW QUIZ 6-2

PAGE 6

Date	Account Titles and Description	PR	Dr.	Cr.

AUXILIARY PETTY CASH RECORD

Date	Voucher No.	Description	Receipts	Payment	Category of Payment				
					Delivery Expense	General Expense	Amount		Sundry

YOU MAKE THE CALL: CRITICAL THINKING/ETHICAL CASE

_____
_____
_____
_____
_____
_____
_____
_____
_____
_____
_____
_____
_____
_____
_____
_____
_____
_____
_____
_____
_____
_____
_____
_____
_____
_____
_____
_____
_____
_____
_____
_____
_____
_____
_____
_____
_____
_____
_____
_____
_____

CHAPTER 6
FORMS FOR MINI EXERCISES

1.

    A, _____   E. _____

    B. _____   F. _____

    C. _____

    D. _____

2.

3.   _____   _____   _____   _____

WOODY CO.
BANK RECONCILIATION
MAY 31, 19XX

Checkbook	Bank

4.

    A. ____ ____ ____   E. ____ ____ ____

    B. ____ ____ ____   F. ____ ____ ____

    C. ____ ____ ____

    D. ____ ____ ____

5.

6.

FORMS FOR EXERCISES

6-1.

NORRY CO.
BANK RECONCILIATION AS OF JULY 31, 19XX

CHECKBOOK BALANCE		BALANCE PER BANK	
Ending Checkbook Balance	_____	Ending Bank Statement Balance	_____
Deduct:	_____	Add:	_____
Bank Service Charge	_____	Deposit in Transit	_____
	_____		
	_____	Deduct:	_____
	_____	Outstanding Checks	_____
Reconciled Balance	_____	Reconciled Balance	_____

6-2.

6-3.

EXERCISES (CONTINUED)

6-4.

6-5.

Beg. Change Fund	_____
+ Cash Register Total	_____
= Cash should have on hand	_____
- Counted Cash	_____
= Cash Shortage	_____

END OF CHAPTER PROBLEMS

PROBLEM 6A-1 OR PROBLEM 6B-1

ROSE COMPANY
BANK RECONCILIATION AS OF JULY 31, 19XX

BALANCE PER BANK

Bank Statement Balance

   Add:

   Deduct:

Reconciled Balance

CHECKBOOK BALANCE

Checkbook Balance

   Add:

   Deduct:

Reconciled Balance

PROBLEM 6A-1 OR PROBLEM 6B-1 (CONCLUDED)

Date		Account Titles and Description	PR	Dr.	Cr.

PROBLEM 6A-2 OR PROBLEM 6B-2

JAMES NATIONAL BANK
RIO MEAN BRAND
BUGNA, TEXAS   Telephone 555-8311

This form is provided to help you balance your bank statement. If no errors are reported to auditors in ten days, the account will be considered correct.

Please notify us of any change in address.

Checks outstanding
(not charged to account)

Check No.	Amount
Total	

Sort the checks numerically or
by date issued.
Check off on the stubs of your
checkbook each check paid by bank.
List the numbers and amounts of
checks still outstanding in the
space provided at the left.
Verify the deposits in your checkbook with
deposits credited on this statement. Bank
balance show on this statement $_____
Plus: Deposits not
      credited on this statement $_____
            Subtotal $_____
Less: Checks outstanding $_____
Balance $_____

If your checkbook does not agree, enter any
necessary adjustments:

Correct checkbook balance $_____

PROBLEM 6A-2 OR PROBLEM 6B-2 (CONCLUDED)

GENERAL JOURNAL

Date		Account Titles and Description	PR	Dr.	Cr.

PROBLEM 6A-3 OR PROBLEM 6B-3

MERRY CO.
GENERAL JOURNAL

PAGE 33

Date		Account Titles and Description	PR		Dr.			Cr.		

PROBLEM 6A-3 OR PROBLEM 6B-3 (CONCLUDED)

MERRY CO.
AUXILIARY PETTY CASH RECORD

Date	Voucher No.	Description	Receipts	Payment	Category of Payment				
					Postage Expense	Office Supplies Expense	Account	Sundry Amount	

PROBLEM 6A-4 OR PROBLEM 6B-4

LOGAN CO.
GENERAL JOURNAL

Date		Account Titles and Description	PR		Dr.			Cr.	

PROBLEM 6A-4 OR PROBLEM 6B-4

LOGAN CO.
AUXILIARY PETTY CASH RECORD

Date	Voucher No.	Description	Receipts	Payment	Category of Payment				
					Postage Expense	Delivery Expense	Account	Sundry	Amount

CHAPTER 6
SUMMARY PRACTICE TEST
BANKING PROCEDURES AND CONTROL OF CASH

Part I Instructions

Fill in the blank(s) to complete the statement.

1. _____ _____ limit any further negotiations of a check.

2. Deposits in transit are _____ to the bank balance.

3. All adjustments to the checkbook balance in the reconciliation process will require_____ _____.

4. Petty cash is an _____ found on the balance sheet.

5. The auxiliary petty cash record is not a _____.

6. A _____ _____ is an asset used to make change for customer.

7. A cash overage will be _____ _____ on the income statement.

8. _____ _____ represents checks not processed by the bank at the time the bank statement was prepared.

9. When a bank debits your account, your balance will _____.

10. _____ is a procedure whereby the bank does not return the processed checks.

Part II Instructions

Indicate which of the following procedures are involved in each of the transactions below.

a. Recorded in General Journal
b. Recorded in both general journal and auxiliary petty cash record
c. Recorded only in auxiliary petty cash record
d. New check is written
e. Account petty cash is increased

1. EXAMPLE: Check issued to establish petty cash   b,d,e

2. Paid donation from petty cash   _____

3. Paid postage from petty cash   _____

4. Paid past purchases previously charged   _____

5. Paid for business luncheon with petty cash   _____

6. Issued check to pay for office supplies   _____

7. Replenished petty cash   _____

8. Paid local donation from petty cash   _____

9. Paid for past purchases bought on account   _____

10. Replenished petty cash   _____

Part III Instructions

Answer true or false to the following statements.

1. Checks outstanding have reached the bank but have not been recorded in the checkbook.
2. Petty cash is a liability found on the balance sheet.
3. Checks returned from the bank are placed in alphabetical order.
4. The General Journal has a record of all checks written.
5. Bank service charges represent an expense to business.
6. The bank statement is the same as the bank reconciliation.
7. The balance in the company cash account will always equal the bank balance before the bank statement is received.
8. Deposit slips are needed in writing checks.
9. The signature must be presented when cashing a check.
10. The auxiliary petty cash record is posted monthly.
11. The petty cash account has a debit balance.
12. Replenishment of petty cash requires a new check.
13. The expenses paid from petty cash are journalized at time of replenishment.
14. Internal control only affects large companies.
15. A petty cash voucher records the expense into the ledger.
16. The petty cash fund must be replenished monthly.
17. The petty cash voucher identifies the account that will be charged.
18. The establishment of petty cash may require some judgment as to the amount of petty cash needed.
19. EFT is the same as safekeeping.
20. The drawer is the person who receives the check.
21. A debit memo will increase the depositor's balance.
22. A change fund uses only one denomination.
23. The payer is the person or company the check is payable to.

Part IV Instructions

Based on the following situation, prepare a bank reconciliation.
The checkbook balance of Moore Company is $3,763.08. The bank statement shows a bank balance of $6,480. The bank statement shows interest earned of $42 and a service charge of $29.76. There is a deposit in transit of $2,558.22. Outstanding checks total $3,762.90. The bank collected a note for Moore for $4,200. Moore Company forgot to deduct a check for $2,700 during the month.

SOLUTIONS TO SUMMARY PRACTICE TEST

Part I

1. restrictive endorsements
2. added
3. journal entries
4. asset
5. journal

6. change fund
7. miscellaneous income
8. checks outstanding
9. decrease
10. safekeeping

Part II

1. b, d, e
2. c
3. c
4. a, d
5. c

6. a, d
7. b, d
8. c
9. a, d
10. b, d

Part III

1. false
2. false
3. false
4. false
5. true

6. false
7. false
8. false
9. true
10. false

11. true
12. true
13. true
14. false
15. false

16. false
17. true
18. true
19. false
20. false

21. false
22. false
23. false

Part IV

MOORE CO.			BANK BALANCE	
Checkbook Balance		$3,763.08	Bank Balance	$6,480.00
ADD:			ADD:	
			Deposit	
Interest	$ 42		in Transit	2,558.22
Collection of note	4,200	4,242.00		$9,038.22
		8,005.08		
DEDUCT:			DEDUCT:	
Service Chg.	$ 29.76		Check outstanding	$3,762.90
Error	2,700.00	2,729.76		
Reconciled Balance		$5,275.32	Reconciled Balance	$5,275.32

CHAPTERS 1-6
ACCOUNTING RECALL FORMS

Part I

1. _____   6. _____

2. _____   7. _____

3. _____   8. _____

4. _____   9. _____

5. _____   10. _____

Part II

11. _____

12. _____

13. _____

14. _____

15. _____

CONTINUING PROBLEM FOR CHAPTER 6

ELDORADO COMPUTER CENTER
GENERAL JOURNAL

PAGE 3

Date	Account Titles and Description	PR	Dr.	Cr.

CASH ACCOUNT NO. **1000**

Date	Explanation	Post Ref.	Debit	Credit	Balance Debit	Balance Credit
9/30 XX	Balance forward	√			1 6 4 5 00	

PETTY CASH ACCOUNT NO. **1010**

Date	Explanation	Post Ref.	Debit	Credit	Balance Debit	Balance Credit

ACCOUNTS RECEIVABLE   ACCOUNT NO. 1020

Date		Explanation	Post Ref.	Debit	Credit	Balance Debit	Balance Credit
9/30	XX	Balance forward	√			2 6 0 0 00	

PREPAID RENT   ACCOUNT NO. 1025

Date		Explanation	Post Ref.	Debit	Credit	Balance Debit	Balance Credit
9/30	XX	Balance forward	√			4 0 0 00	

SUPPLIES   ACCOUNT NO. 1030

Date		Explanation	Post Ref.	Debit	Credit	Balance Debit	Balance Credit
9/30	XX	Balance forward	√			9 0 00	

COMPUTER SHOP EQUIPMENT   ACCOUNT NO. 1080

Date		Explanation	Post Ref.	Debit	Credit	Balance Debit	Balance Credit
9/30	XX	Balance forward	√			2 4 0 0 00	

ACCUMULATED DEPRECIATION, COMPUTER SHOP EQUIPMENT   ACCOUNT NO. <u>1081</u>

Date		Explanation	Post Ref.	Debit	Credit	Balance	
						Debit	Credit
9/30	XX	Balance forward	√				9 9

OFFICE EQUIPMENT   ACCOUNT NO. <u>1090</u>

Date		Explanation	Post Ref.	Debit	Credit	Balance	
						Debit	Credit
9/30	XX	Balance forward	√			6 0 0 00	

ACCUMULATED DEPRECIATION, OFFICE EQUIPMENT   ACCOUNT NO. <u>1091</u>

Date		Explanation	Post Ref.	Debit	Credit	Balance	
						Debit	Credit
9/30	XX	Balance forward	√				2 0 00

ACCOUNTS PAYABLE   ACCOUNT NO. <u>2000</u>

Date		Explanation	Post Ref.	Debit	Credit	Balance	
						Debit	Credit
9/30	XX	Balance forward	√				2 1 0 00

T. FREEDMAN, CAPITAL   ACCOUNT NO. **3000**

Date		Explanation	Post Ref.	Debit	Credit	Balance Debit	Balance Credit
9/30	XX	Balance forward	√				7 4 0 6 00

T. FREEDMAN, WITHDRAWALS   ACCOUNT NO. **3010**

Date	Explanation	Post Ref.	Debit	Credit	Balance Debit	Balance Credit

INCOME SUMMARY   ACCOUNT NO. **3020**

Date	Explanation	Post Ref.	Debit	Credit	Balance Debit	Balance Credit

SERVICE REVENUE ACCOUNT NO. <u>4000</u>

Date		Explanation	Post Ref.	Debit	Credit	Balance	
						Debit	Credit

ADVERTISING EXPENSE ACCOUNT NO. <u>5010</u>

Date		Explanation	Post Ref.	Debit	Credit	Balance	
						Debit	Credit

RENT EXPENSE ACCOUNT NO. <u>5020</u>

Date		Explanation	Post Ref.	Debit	Credit	Balance	
						Debit	Credit

UTILITIES EXPENSE   ACCOUNT NO. <u>5030</u>

Date	Explanation	Post Ref.	Debit	Credit	Balance Debit	Balance Credit

PHONE EXPENSE   ACCOUNT NO. <u>5040</u>

Date	Explanation	Post Ref.	Debit	Credit	Balance Debit	Balance Credit

SUPPLIES EXPENSE   ACCOUNT NO. <u>5050</u>

Date	Explanation	Post Ref.	Debit	Credit	Balance Debit	Balance Credit

INSURANCE EXPENSE   ACCOUNT NO. <u>5060</u>

Date	Explanation	Post Ref.	Debit	Credit	Balance Debit	Balance Credit

POSTAGE EXPENSE   ACCOUNT NO. 5070

Date	Explanation	Post Ref.	Debit	Credit	Balance Debit	Balance Credit

DEPRECIATION EXPENSE, COMPUTER SHOP EQUIPMENT   ACCOUNT NO. 5080

Date	Explanation	Post Ref.	Debit	Credit	Balance Debit	Balance Credit

DEPRECIATION EXPENSE, OFFICE EQUIPMENT   ACCOUNT NO. 5090

Date	Explanation	Post Ref.	Debit	Credit	Balance Debit	Balance Credit

MISCELLANEOUS EXPENSE   ACCOUNT NO. 5100

Date	Explanation	Post Ref.	Debit	Credit	Balance Debit	Balance Credit

ELDORADO COMPUTER CENTER
TRIAL BALANCE
OCTOBER 31, 19XX

AUXILIARY PETTY CASH RECORD

Date	Voucher No.	Description	Receipts	Payment	Postage Expense	Supplies	Account	Sundry Amount

Category of Payment

ELDORADO COMPUTER CENTER
BANK RECONCILIATION AS OF SEPTEMBER 30, 19XX

BALANCE PER BANK

Bank Statement Balance

  Add:

  Deduct:

Reconciled Balance

CHECKBOOK BALANCE

Checkbook Balance

  Add:

  Deduct:

Reconciled Balance

SOLUTIONS TO ACCOUNTING RECALL

Part I

1.	D	**6.**	C
2.	J	**7.**	A
3.	E	**8.**	G
4.	B	**9.**	H
5.	I	**10.**	F

Part II

11. False; Asset

12. False; Not a Journal

13. True

14. False; Checkbook Balance

15. True

PAYROLL CONCEPTS AND PROCEDURES— EMPLOYEE TAXES

SELF-REVIEW QUIZ 7-1
FICA (Social Security and Medicare)

_____
_____
_____
_____

Federal Income Tax

_____
_____
_____
_____

State Income Tax

_____
_____
_____

SELF-REVIEW QUIZ 7-2
FICA (Social Security and Medicare)

_____
_____
_____
_____

Federal Income Tax

_____
_____
_____

State Income Tax

_____
_____
_____

Net Pay

_____
_____

SELF-REVIEW QUIZ 7-3

1. _____ 2. _____ 3. _____ 4. _____ 5. _____

YOU MAKE THE CALL: CRITICAL THINKING/ETHICAL CASE

_____
_____
_____
_____
_____
_____
_____
_____
_____
_____
_____
_____
_____
_____
_____
_____
_____
_____
_____
_____
_____
_____
_____
_____
_____
_____
_____
_____
_____
_____
_____
_____
_____
_____
_____
_____
_____
_____
_____
_____
_____
_____
_____
_____
_____

FORMS FOR CHAPTER 7
MINI EXERCISES

1. A
   _____
   _____
   _____

   B.
   _____
   _____
   _____

2.
   _____
   _____
   _____
   _____

3.
   _____
   _____
   _____
   _____

4. A. _____ D. _____
   B. _____ E. _____
   C. _____ F. _____

5.
   A. _____
   B. _____
   C. _____
   D. _____
   E. _____

FORMS FOR EXERCISES

7-1.

Bob Role   _____

Jill West   _____
_____

Dale Aster _____
_____

7-2. _____

_____
_____
_____
_____
_____
_____
_____
_____
_____
_____

7-3.

ACCOUNT	CATEGORY	↑ NORMAL BALANCE	REPORT FOUND ON

7-4. _____

_____
_____
_____
_____
_____
_____

7-5.

END OF CHAPTER PROBLEMS

PROBLEM 7A-1 OR PROBLEM 7B-1

Employee	Hourly Rate	# of Hours Worked	Gross Earnings
A.			
B.			
C.			
D.			

A.   B.

C.   D.

PROBLEM 7A-2 OR PROBLEM 7B-2

Use the fold-out payroll register located at the end of this study guide.

PROBLEM 7A-3 OR PROBLEM 7B-3

Use the fold-out payroll register located at the end of this study guide.

PROBLEM 7A-3 OR PROBLEM 7B-3 (CONCLUDED)

GENERAL JOURNAL

PROBLEM 7A-4 OR PROBLEM 7B-4

Use the fold-out payroll register located at the end of this study guide.

PROBLEM 7A-4 OR PROBLEM 7B-4 (CONTINUED)

GENERAL JOURNAL

PAGE 4

Date		Account Titles and Description	PR		Dr.		Cr.

PROBLEM 7A-4 OR PROBLEM 7B-4 (CONTINUED)

PARTIAL GENERAL LEDGER

FICA—SOCIAL SECURITY PAYABLE　　　　**ACCOUNT NO. 210**

Date	Explanation	Post Ref.	Debit	Credit	Balance Debit	Balance Credit

FICA—MEDICARE PAYABLE　　　　**ACCOUNT NO. 212**

Date	Explanation	Post Ref.	Debit	Credit	Balance Debit	Balance Credit

FIT PAYABLE　　　　**ACCOUNT NO. 214**

Date	Explanation	Post Ref.	Debit	Credit	Balance Debit	Balance Credit

SIT PAYABLE　　　　**ACCOUNT NO. 216**

Date	Explanation	Post Ref.	Debit	Credit	Balance Debit	Balance Credit

PROBLEM 7A-4 OR PROBLEM 7B-4 (CONCLUDED)

UNION DUES PAYABLE   ACCOUNT NO. 218

Date	Explanation	Post Ref.	Debit	Credit	Balance Debit	Balance Credit

WAGES AND SALARIES PAYABLE   ACCOUNT NO. 220

Date	Explanation	Post Ref.	Debit	Credit	Balance Debit	Balance Credit

FACTORY SALARIES EXPENSE   ACCOUNT NO. 610

Date	Explanation	Post Ref.	Debit	Credit	Balance Debit	Balance Credit

OFFICE SALARIES EXPENSE   ACCOUNT NO. 612

Date	Explanation	Post Ref.	Debit	Credit	Balance Debit	Balance Credit

CHAPTER 7
SUMMARY PRACTICE TEST:
PAYROLL CONCEPTS AND PROCEDURES—EMPLOYEE TAXES

Part I Instructions

Fill in the blank (s) to complete the statement.

1. The _____ _____ _____
   _____ states the maximum hours a worker will work at regular rate of pay.

2. Form _____ aids the employer in knowing how much to deduct for federal income tax.

3. The base for FICA-Medicare will _____ _____ from year to year.

4. _____ _____ of the employer's tax guide has tables available for deductions for FIT and FICA (Social Security and Medicare).

5. _____ _____ _____ protects employees against losses due to injury or death incurred while on the job.

6. Data from the _____ _____ will provide the needed information to record the payroll entry in the general journal.

7. The _____ _____ _____
   _____ in the payroll register identifies how the total gross earnings are to be charged to specific accounts.

8. The credit to Wages and Salaries Payable in recording the payroll entry in the general journal represents _____ _____.

9. FICA-Social Security Payable is a _____ found on the balance sheet.

10. Each quarter has _____ weeks.

Part II Instructions

Answer true or false to the following.

1. The individual earnings record is updated from the general journal.
2. The account distribution columns of the payroll register provide data to record which accounts will be debited to record the total payroll when a journal entry is prepared.
3. FICA-Medicare Payable is an asset for the employer.
4. Gross pay plus deductions equals net pay.
5. Form W-4 aids in calculating FICA-Social Security.
6. The employer will match the employee's contribution for FICA (Social Security and Medicare).
7. Each quarter has 13 weeks.
8. The normal balance of FIT Payable is a credit.

Name _____ Class _____ Date _____

9. The Wage-Bracket Table makes it more difficult to calculate the amount of deductions for FIT.

10. A calendar year has no effect on taxes for FICA-Social Security.

Part III Instructions

Complete the chart below (use table in text as needed). Use the following information: Before this payroll John Roll had earned $65,300. This week John earned $900. Assume a FICA rate of Social Security of 6.2% on $65,400. Medicare, 1.45%. John is married, claiming one deduction. The state income tax is 7 percent.

GROSS PAY	TAXABLE FICA	DEDUCTIONS		FIT	SIT	NET PAY
		FICA				
		Soc. Sec.	Med.			

CHAPTER 7
SOLUTIONS TO SUMMARY PRACTICE TEST

Part I

1. Fair Labors Standards Act
2. W-4
3. Not change
4. Circular E
5. Workers' Compensation Insurance

6. Payroll register
7. Labor distribution account numbers
8. Net earnings
9. Liability
10. 13

Part II

1. false
2. true
3. false
4. false
5. false

6. true
7. true
8. true
9. false
10. false

Part III

FICA			
Social Security	$100 x .062 =	$ 6.20	
Medicare	900 x .0145 =	13.05	
FIT	by table	117.00	$900.00
SIT	900 x .07	63.00	- 199.25
Total deductions		$199.25	$700.75

CHAPTERS 1-7
ACCOUNTING RECALL FORMS

Part I

1. _____   6. _____

2. _____   7. _____

3. _____   8. _____

4. _____   9. _____

5. _____   10. _____

Part II

11. _____

12. _____

13. _____

14. _____

15. _____

Name _____ Class _____ Date _____

CONTINUING PROBLEM FOR CHAPTER 7*

ELDORADO COMPUTER CENTER
GENERAL JOURNAL

Date	Account Titles and Description	PR	Dr.	Cr.

*Payroll register is located in envelope at end of study guide/working papers.

ELDORADO COMPUTER CENTER
GENERAL JOURNAL

PAGE 5

Date	Account Titles and Description	PR	Dr.	Cr.

CASH   ACCOUNT NO. 1000

Date		Explanation	Post Ref.	Debit	Credit	Balance	
						Debit	Credit
10/31	XX	Balance forward	√			4 2 9 3 00	

PETTY CASH   ACCOUNT NO. 1010

Date		Explanation	Post Ref.	Debit	Credit	Balance	
						Debit	Credit
10/31	XX	Balance forward	√			1 0 0 00	

ACCOUNTS RECEIVABLE   ACCOUNT NO. 1020

Date		Explanation	Post Ref.	Debit	Credit	Balance	
						Debit	Credit
10/31	XX	Balance forward	√			4 2 0 0 00	

PREPAID RENT   ACCOUNT NO. 1025

Date		Explanation	Post Ref.	Debit	Credit	Balance Debit	Balance Credit
10/31	XX	Balance forward	√			1 6 0 0 00	

SUPPLIES   ACCOUNT NO. 1030

Date		Explanation	Post Ref.	Debit	Credit	Balance Debit	Balance Credit
10/31	XX	Balance forward	√			1 3 2 00	

COMPUTER SHOP EQUIPMENT   ACCOUNT NO. 1080

Date		Explanation	Post Ref.	Debit	Credit	Balance Debit	Balance Credit
10/31	XX	Balance forward	√			2 4 0 0 00	

ACCUMULATED DEPRECIATION, COMPUTER SHOP EQUIPMENT ACCOUNT NO. 1081

Date		Explanation	Post Ref.	Debit	Credit	Balance Debit	Balance Credit
10/31	XX	Balance forward	√				9 9 00

OFFICE EQUIPMENT   ACCOUNT NO. 1090

Date		Explanation	Post Ref.	Debit	Credit	Balance Debit	Balance Credit
10/31	XX	Balance forward	√			6 0 0 00	

ACCUMULATED DEPRECIATION, OFFICE EQUIPMENT   ACCOUNT NO. 1091

Date		Explanation	Post Ref.	Debit	Credit	Balance Debit	Balance Credit
10/31	XX	Balance forward	√				2 0 00

ACCOUNTS PAYABLE   ACCOUNT NO. 2000

Date		Explanation	Post Ref.	Debit	Credit	Balance Debit	Balance Credit
10/31	XX	Balance forward	√				5 0 00

WAGES PAYABLE   ACCOUNT NO. 2010

Date		Explanation	Post Ref.	Debit	Credit	Balance Debit	Balance Credit

PARTIAL GENERAL LEDGER

FICA—SOCIAL SECURITY PAYABLE ACCOUNT NO. 2020

Date	Explanation	Post Ref.	Debit	Credit	Balance Debit	Balance Credit

FICA—MEDICARE PAYABLE ACCOUNT NO. 2030

Date	Explanation	Post Ref.	Debit	Credit	Balance Debit	Balance Credit

FIT PAYABLE ACCOUNT NO. 2040

Date	Explanation	Post Ref.	Debit	Credit	Balance Debit	Balance Credit

SIT PAYABLE ACCOUNT NO. 2050

Date	Explanation	Post Ref.	Debit	Credit	Balance Debit	Balance Credit

T. FREEDMAN CAPITAL   ACCOUNT NO. 3000

Date		Explanation	Post Ref.	Debit	Credit	Balance Debit	Balance Credit
10/31	XX	Balance forward	√				7 4 0 6 00

T. FREEDMAN WITHDRAWALS   ACCOUNT NO.

Date		Explanation	Post Ref.	Debit	Credit	Balance Debit	Balance Credit
10/31	XX	Balance forward	√			2 0 1 5 00	

SERVICE REVENUE   ACCOUNT NO. 4000

Date		Explanation	Post Ref.	Debit	Credit	Balance Debit	Balance Credit
10/31	XX	Balance forward	√				7 8 0 0 00

ADVERTISING EXPENSE   ACCOUNT NO. 5010

Date		Explanation	Post Ref.	Debit	Credit	Balance Debit	Balance Credit

RENT EXPENSE   ACCOUNT NO. 5020

Date		Explanation	Post Ref.	Debit	Credit	Balance Debit	Balance Credit

UTILITIES EXPENSE ACCOUNT NO. 5030

Date	Explanation	Post Ref.	Debit	Credit	Balance Debit	Balance Credit

PHONE EXPENSE ACCOUNT NO. 5040

Date	Explanation	Post Ref.	Debit	Credit	Balance Debit	Balance Credit

SUPPLIES EXPENSE ACCOUNT NO. 5050

Date	Explanation	Post Ref.	Debit	Credit	Balance Debit	Balance Credit

INSURANCE EXPENSE ACCOUNT NO. 5060

Date	Explanation	Post Ref.	Debit	Credit	Balance Debit	Balance Credit

POSTAGE EXPENSE ACCOUNT NO. 5070

Date	Explanation	Post Ref.	Debit	Credit	Balance Debit	Balance Credit
10/31 XX	Balance forward	√			2 5 00	

DEPRECIATION EXPENSE C. S. EQUIPMENT   ACCOUNT NO. 5080

Date		Explanation	Post Ref.	Debit	Credit	Balance Debit	Balance Credit

DEPRECIATION EXPENSE OFFICE EQUIPMENT   ACCOUNT NO. 5090

Date		Explanation	Post Ref.	Debit	Credit	Balance Debit	Balance Credit

MISCELLANEOUS EXPENSE   ACCOUNT NO. 5100

Date		Explanation	Post Ref.	Debit	Credit	Balance Debit	Balance Credit
10/31	XX	Balance Forward				1 0 00	

WAGES EXPENSE   ACCOUNT NO. 5110

Date 19XX		Explanation	Post Ref.	Debit	Credit	Balance Debit	Balance Credit

ELDORADO COMPUTER CENTER
TRIAL BALANCE
NOVEMBER 30, 19XX

		Dr.		Cr.	

SOLUTIONS TO ACCOUNTING RECALL

Part I

1. E
2. D
3. G
4. H
5. I

6. B
7. F
8. A
9. J
10. C

Part II

11. False
12. False; Supplementary Record
13. True
14. False; Net Pay
15. True

8

THE EMPLOYERS TAX RESPONSIBILITIES: PRINCIPLES AND PROCEDURES

SELF-REVIEW QUIZ 8-1

GENERAL JOURNAL

Date		Account Titles and Description	PR		Dr.			Cr.	

SELF-REVIEW QUIZ 8-2

1.

2.

SELF-REVIEW QUIZ 8-3

1. _____ 2. _____ 3. _____ 4. _____ 5. _____ 6. _____

YOU MAKE THE CALL: CRITICAL THINKING/ETHICAL CASE

_____

_____

_____

_____

_____

_____

_____

_____

_____

_____

_____

_____

_____

_____

_____

_____

_____

_____

_____

_____

_____

_____

_____

_____

_____

_____

_____

_____

_____

_____

_____

_____

_____

_____

_____

_____

_____

_____

_____

_____

_____

_____

FORMS FOR MINI EXERCISES

1.

A.			
B.			
C.			
D.			
E.			

2.

_____
_____
_____
_____

3.

A. _____
B. _____
C. _____
D. _____

4.

_____
_____
_____
_____

5.

A. _____
B. _____
C. _____
D. _____
E. _____
F. _____
G. _____

FORMS FOR EXERCISES

8-1.

8-2.

8-3.

EXERCISES (CONTINUED)

8-4.

_____

_____

_____

_____

_____

_____

_____

8-5.

_____

_____

_____

_____

8-6.

_____

_____

8-7.

_____

_____

8-8.

EXERCISES (CONTINUED)

8-9.

8-10.

END OF CHAPTER PROBLEMS

PROBLEM 8A-1 OR PROBLEM 8B-1

Employee	Allowance & Marital Status	Gross	FICA		Federal Income Tax
			Soc. Sec.	Medicare	

(2)

PROBLEM 8A-2 OR PROBLEM 8B-2

Date		Account Titles and Description	PR	Dr.	Cr.

PROBLEM 8A-2 OR PROBLEM 8B-2 (CONCLUDED)

Date	Account Titles and Description	PR	Dr.	Cr.

PROBLEM 8A-3 OR PROBLEM 8B-3

Form **941**
(Rev. January 199X)
Department of the Treasury
Internal Revenue Service (O)

4141

Employer's Quarterly Federal Tax Return

▶ See separate instructions for information on completing this return.

Please type or print.

Name (as distinguished from trade name)	Date quarter ended
Trade name, if any	Employer identification number
Address (number and street)	City, state, and ZIP code

OMB No. 1545-0029

T
FF
FD
FP
I
T

Enter state code for state in which deposits made . ▶ ⬚

(see page 3 of instructions).

If address is different from prior return, check here ▶ ⬚

IRS Use

1 1 1 1 1 1 1 1 1 1   2   3 3 3 3 3 3   4 4 4

5 5 5   6   7   8 8 8 8 8   9 9 9   10 10 10 10 10 10 10 10 10 10

If you do not have to file returns in the future, check here ▶ ⬚ and enter date final wages paid ▶ _____

If you are a seasonal employer, see **Seasonal employers** on page 1 of the instructions and check here ▶ ⬚

1	Number of employees (except household) employed in the pay period that includes March 12th ▶	**1**
2	Total wages and tips, plus other compensation	**2**
3	Total income tax withheld from wages, tips, and sick pay	**3**
4	Adjustment of withheld income tax for preceding quarters of calendar year	**4**
5	Adjusted total of income tax withheld (line 3 as adjusted by line 4—see instructions) . . .	**5**
6	Taxable social security wages . . . . . 6a $ _____ × 12.4% (.124) =	**6b**
	Taxable social security tips . . . . . . 6c $ _____ × 12.4% (.124) =	**6d**
7	Taxable Medicare wages and tips . . . 7a $ _____ × 2.9% (.029) =	**7b**
8	Total social security and Medicare taxes (add lines 6b, 6d, and 7b). Check here if wages are not subject to social security and/or Medicare tax . . . . ▶ ⬚	**8**
9	Adjustment of social security and Medicare taxes (see instructions for required explanation) Sick Pay $ _____ ± Fractions of Cents $ _____ ± Other $ _____ =	**9**
10	Adjusted total of social security and Medicare taxes (line 8 as adjusted by line 9—see instructions)	**10**
11	**Total taxes** (add lines 5 and 10)	**11**
12	Advance earned income credit (EIC) payments made to employees	**12**
13	Net taxes (subtract line 12 from line 11). **This should equal line 17, column (d) below** (or line D of Schedule B (Form 941))	**13**
14	Total deposits for quarter, including overpayment applied from a prior quarter	**14**
15	**Balance due** (subtract line 14 from line 13). See instructions	**15**
16	**Overpayment,** if line 14 is more than line 13, enter excess here ▶ $ _____	

and check if to be: ⬚ Applied to next return **OR** ⬚ Refunded.

- **All filers:** If line 13 is less than $500, you need not complete line 17 or Schedule B.
- **Semiweekly schedule depositors:** Complete Schedule B and check here . . . . ▶ ⬚
- **Monthly schedule depositors:** Complete line 17, columns (a) through (d), and check here . . . . ▶ ⬚

17	**Monthly Summary of Federal Tax Liability**			
	(a) First month liability	(b) Second month liability	(c) Third month liability	(d) Total liability for quarter

Sign Here

Under penalties of perjury, I declare that I have examined this return, including accompanying schedules and statements, and to the best of my knowledge and belief, it is true, correct, and complete.

Signature ▶ _____ Print Your Name and Title ▶ _____ Date ▶ _____

For Paperwork Reduction Act Notice, see page 1 of separate instructions.   Cat. No. 17001Z   Form **941** (Rev. 1-97)

PROBLEM 8A-4 OR PROBLEM 8B-4

Form **941**
(Rev. January 199X)
Department of the Treasury
Internal Revenue Service   (O)

4141

Employer's Quarterly Federal Tax Return

▶ See separate instructions for information on completing this return.

Please type or print.

Enter state code for state in which deposits made . ▶ ☐
(see page 3 of instructions).

Name (as distinguished from trade name)	Date quarter ended
Trade name, if any	Employer identification number
Address (number and street)	City, state, and ZIP code

OMB No. 1545-0029

| T |
| FF |
| FD |
| FP |
| I |
| T |

If address is different from prior return, check here ▶ ☐

IRS Use

| 1 1 1 1 1 1 1 1 1 1 | 2 | 3 3 3 3 3 3 | 4 4 4 |
| 5 5 5 | 6 | 7 | 8 8 8 8 8 | 9 9 9 | 10 10 10 10 | 10 10 10 10 10 10 |

If you do not have to file returns in the future, check here ▶ ☐   and enter date final wages paid ▶

If you are a seasonal employer, see **Seasonal employers** on page 1 of the instructions and check here ▶ ☐

1	Number of employees (except household) employed in the pay period that includes March 12th ▶	**1**
2	Total wages and tips, plus other compensation	**2**
3	Total income tax withheld from wages, tips, and sick pay	**3**
4	Adjustment of withheld income tax for preceding quarters of calendar year	**4**
5	Adjusted total of income tax withheld (line 3 as adjusted by line 4—see instructions) . . .	**5**
6	Taxable social security wages . . . . . 6a $ _____ × 12.4% (.124) =	**6b**
	Taxable social security tips . . . . . . 6c $ _____ × 12.4% (.124) =	**6d**
7	Taxable Medicare wages and tips . . . 7a $ _____ × 2.9% (.029) =	**7b**
8	Total social security and Medicare taxes (add lines 6b, 6d, and 7b). Check here if wages are not subject to social security and/or Medicare tax . . . . ▶ ☐	**8**
9	Adjustment of social security and Medicare taxes (see instructions for required explanation) Sick Pay $ _____ ± Fractions of Cents $ _____ ± Other $ _____ =	**9**
10	Adjusted total of social security and Medicare taxes (line 8 as adjusted by line 9—see instructions)	**10**
11	**Total taxes** (add lines 5 and 10)	**11**
12	Advance earned income credit (EIC) payments made to employees	**12**
13	Net taxes (subtract line 12 from line 11). **This should equal line 17, column (d) below** (or line D of Schedule B (Form 941))	**13**
14	Total deposits for quarter, including overpayment applied from a prior quarter	**14**
15	**Balance due** (subtract line 14 from line 13). See instructions	**15**
16	**Overpayment,** if line 14 is more than line 13, enter excess here ▶ $ _____	

and check if to be: ☐ Applied to next return **OR** ☐ Refunded.

- **All filers:** If line 13 is less than $500, you need not complete line 17 or Schedule B.
- **Semiweekly schedule depositors:** Complete Schedule B and check here . . . . ▶ ☐
- **Monthly schedule depositors:** Complete line 17, columns (a) through (d), and check here . . . . ▶ ☐

17	**Monthly Summary of Federal Tax Liability**		
(a) First month liability	**(b)** Second month liability	**(c)** Third month liability	**(d)** Total liability for quarter

Sign Here

Under penalties of perjury, I declare that I have examined this return, including accompanying schedules and statements, and to the best of my knowledge and belief, it is true, correct, and complete.

Signature ▶ _____ Print Your Name and Title ▶ _____ Date ▶ _____

For Paperwork Reduction Act Notice, see page 1 of separate instructions.   Cat. No. 17001Z   Form **941** (Rev. 1-97)

Form **940-EZ**

Department of the Treasury
Internal Revenue Service   (O)

Employer's Annual Federal Unemployment (FUTA) Tax Return

▶ **For Paperwork Reduction Act Notice, see page 4.**

OMB No. 1545-1110

199X

Name (as distinguished from trade name)	Calendar year	T
		FF
Trade name, if any		FD
		FP
Address and ZIP code	Employer identification number	I
		T

*Follow the chart under **Who May Use Form 940-EZ** on page 2. If you cannot use Form 940-EZ, you must use Form 940 instead.*

A Enter the amount of contributions paid to your state unemployment fund. (See instructions for line A on page 4.)▶ $ ....

B (1) Enter the name of the state where you have to pay contributions . . . . ▶ ....

    (2) Enter your state reporting number as shown on state unemployment tax return ▶

If you will not have to file returns in the future, check here (see **Who must file** on page 2) **and complete and sign the return** . . . . ▶ ☐

If this is an Amended Return, check here . . . . ▶ ☐

Part I   Taxable Wages and FUTA Tax

1 Total payments (including payments shown on lines 2 and 3) during the calendar year for services of employees	**1**	

	Amount paid	
2 Exempt payments. (Explain all exempt payments, attaching additional sheets if necessary.) ▶	**2**	
3 Payments for services of more than $7,000. Enter only amounts over the first $7,000 paid to each employee. Do not include any exempt payments from line 2. Do not use your state wage limitation. The $7,000 amount is the Federal wage base. Your state wage base may be different	**3**	

4 Total exempt payments (add lines 2 and 3) **4**

5 **Total taxable wages** (subtract line 4 from line 1) . . . . ▶ **5**

6 **FUTA tax.** Multiply the wages on line 5 by .008 and enter here. (If the result is over $100, also complete Part II.) . **6**

7 Total FUTA tax deposited for the year, including any overpayment applied from a prior year (from your records) **7**

8 **Amount you owe** (subtract line 7 from line 6). This should be $100 or less. Pay to "Internal Revenue Service." ▶ **8**

9 **Overpayment** (subtract line 6 from line 7). Check if it is to be: ☐ **Applied to next return** or ☐ **Refunded** ▶ **9**

Part II   Record of Quarterly Federal Unemployment Tax Liability (Do not include state liability.) Complete only if line 6 is over $100.

Quarter	First (Jan. 1 – Mar. 31)	Second (Apr. 1 – June 30)	Third (July 1 – Sept. 30)	Fourth (Oct. 1 – Dec. 31)	Total for year
Liability for quarter					

Under penalties of perjury, I declare that I have examined this return, including accompanying schedules and statements, and, to the best of my knowledge and belief, it is true, correct, and complete, and that no part of any payment made to a state unemployment fund claimed as a credit was, or is to be, deducted from the payments to employees.

CHAPTER 8
SUMMARY PRACTICE TEST:
THE EMPLOYER'S TAX RESPONSIBILITIES—
PRINCIPLES AND PROCEDURES

Part I Instructions

Fill in the blank(s) to complete the statement.

1. Only the _____ completes the SS-4 Form.
2. The payroll tax expense for the employer is made up of _____, _____, and FUTA.
3. The employer is responsible for paying for_____.
4. SUTA is usually paid _____.
5. FUTA Payable is a _____ found on the _____ _____.
6. Form 941 summarizes the taxes owed for _____ and _____.
7. _____ _____ _____ will tell if a deposit is to be made monthly, or semi-weekly for FIT and Social Security.
8. Form _____ is prepared quarterly to summarize tax liabilities for FICA (Social Security and Medicare) and FIT.
9. The _____ _____ _____ _____ is required to be given to employees by January 31 following the year employed.
10. Form 940EZ records the amount of tax liability for _____.

Part II Instructions

Answer true or false to the following.

1. Prepaid Workers' Compensation Insurance is an asset.
2. Workers' compensation need not be estimated at the beginning of the year.
3. Payroll Tax Expense is made up of FICA, SUTA, and FIT.
4. Frequency of deposits relating to Form 941 is based on amount of tax liability in lookback periods.
5. The maximum tax credit for state unemployment tax is .8% against the FUTA tax.
6. The individual earnings record provides the data to prepare W-2's.
7. A tax calendar provides little help to the employer involving the payment of tax liabilities.
8. Form 941 is completed twice a year.
9. A year-end adjusting entry is needed for workers' compensation.
10. Form 8109 relates only to Form 940EZ.

Part III Instructions

Complete the following table:

ACCOUNT	CATEGORY	FOUND ON WHICH REPORT
1. Payroll Tax Expense		
2. FUTA Payable		
3. SUTA Payable		
4. FICA Tax Payable—Medicare		
5. FIT Payable		
6. Office Salaries Expense		

Part IV Instructions

Complete the following table:

	4 QUARTERS LOOK-BACK PERIOD LIABILITY	PAYROLL PAID WEEKLY	TAX PAID BY:
Sit. A	$40,000	October	?
Sit. B	75,000		
		on Wed.	?
		on Thurs.	?
		on Fri	?
		on Sat.	?
		on Sun.	?
		on Mon.	?
		on. Tues.	?

Why is Depositor in Situation A classified as a Monthly Depositor while in Situation B Depositor is classified as Semi-Weekly?

SOLUTIONS TO SUMMARY PRACTICE TEST

Part I

1. Employer
2. FICA (Social Security and Medicare), SUTA
3. FUTA (SUTA)
4. quarterly
5. liability, balance sheet
6. FICA (Social Security and Medicare), FIT
7. Look-Back Periods
8. 941
9. wage and tax statement
10. FUTA

Part II

1. true
2. false
3. false
4. true
5. false

6. true
7. false
8. false
9. true
10. false

Part III

1. Expense; Income Statement
2. Liability; Balance Sheet
3. Liability; Balance Sheet
4. Liability; Balance Sheet
5. Liability; Balance Sheet
6. Expense; Income Statement

Part IV

Situation A	Nov. 15	
B	on Wed.	
	on Thurs.	on Wed. of Week 2
	on Fri.	
	on Sat.	
	on Sun.	Due Fri. of that week
	on Mon.	
	on Tues.	

CHAPTERS 1-8
ACCOUNTING RECALL FORMS

Part I

Part II

1. _____   6. _____

2. _____   7. _____

3. _____   8. _____

4. _____   9. _____

5. _____   10. _____

11. _____

12. _____

13. _____

14. _____

15. _____

Name_____ Class _____ Date _____

CONTINUING PROBLEM FOR CHAPTER 8
ELDORADO COMPUTER CENTER

ELDORADO COMPUTER CENTER
GENERAL JOURNAL

PAGE 9

Date	Account Titles and Description	PR	Dr.	Cr.

Form **941**
(Rev. January 199X)
Department of the Treasury
Internal Revenue Service (O)

4141

Employer's Quarterly Federal Tax Return

▶ See separate instructions for information on completing this return.

Please type or print.

OMB No. 1545-0029

Enter state code for state in which deposits made . ▶ ☐
(see page 3 of instructions).

Name (as distinguished from trade name)	Date quarter ended
Trade name, if any	Employer identification number
Address (number and street)	City, state, and ZIP code

T	
FF	
FD	
FP	
I	
T	

If address is different from prior return, check here ▶ ☐

IRS Use

1 1 1 1 1 1 1 1 1 1	2	3 3 3 3 3 3	4 4 4	
5 5 5	6	7	8 8 8 8 8	9 9 9	10 10 10 10	10 10 10 10 10 10

If you do not have to file returns in the future, check here ▶ ☐ and enter date final wages paid ▶

If you are a seasonal employer, see **Seasonal employers** on page 1 of the instructions and check here ▶ ☐

1	Number of employees (except household) employed in the pay period that includes March 12th ▶	1	
2	Total wages and tips, plus other compensation	2	
3	Total income tax withheld from wages, tips, and sick pay	3	
4	Adjustment of withheld income tax for preceding quarters of calendar year	4	
5	Adjusted total of income tax withheld (line 3 as adjusted by line 4—see instructions) . . .	5	

6	Taxable social security wages	6a	$	× 12.4% (.124) =	6b	
	Taxable social security tips	6c	$	× 12.4% (.124) =	6d	
7	Taxable Medicare wages and tips . . .	7a	$	× 2.9% (.029) =	7b	

8	Total social security and Medicare taxes (add lines 6b, 6d, and 7b). Check here if wages are not subject to social security and/or Medicare tax . . . . ▶ ☐	8	
9	Adjustment of social security and Medicare taxes (see instructions for required explanation) Sick Pay $ _____ ± Fractions of Cents $ _____ ± Other $ _____ =	9	
10	Adjusted total of social security and Medicare taxes (line 8 as adjusted by line 9—see instructions)	10	
11	**Total taxes** (add lines 5 and 10)	11	
12	Advance earned income credit (EIC) payments made to employees	12	
13	Net taxes (subtract line 12 from line 11). **This should equal line 17, column (d) below** (or line D of Schedule B (Form 941))	13	
14	Total deposits for quarter, including overpayment applied from a prior quarter	14	
15	**Balance due** (subtract line 14 from line 13). See instructions	15	

16 **Overpayment,** if line 14 is more than line 13, enter excess here ▶ $ _____
and check if to be: ☐ Applied to next return **OR** ☐ Refunded.

- **All filers:** If line 13 is less than $500, you need not complete line 17 or Schedule B.
- **Semiweekly schedule depositors:** Complete Schedule B and check here . . . . ▶ ☐
- **Monthly schedule depositors:** Complete line 17, columns (a) through (d), and check here . . . . ▶ ☐

17	**Monthly Summary of Federal Tax Liability**		
(a) First month liability	(b) Second month liability	(c) Third month liability	(d) Total liability for quarter

Sign Here

Under penalties of perjury, I declare that I have examined this return, including accompanying schedules and statements, and to the best of my knowledge and belief, it is true, correct, and complete.

Signature ▶   Print Your Name and Title ▶   Date ▶

For Paperwork Reduction Act Notice, see page 1 of separate instructions.   Cat. No. 17001Z   Form **941** (Rev. 1-97)

Form **940-EZ**

Department of the Treasury
Internal Revenue Service   (O)

**Employer's Annual Federal
Unemployment (FUTA) Tax Return**

▶ **For Paperwork Reduction Act Notice, see page 4.**

OMB No. 1545-1110

19**9X**

T	
FF	
FD	
FP	
I	
T	

Name (as distinguished from trade name)		Calendar year
Trade name, if any		
Address and ZIP code		Employer identification number

*Follow the chart under **Who May Use Form 940-EZ** on page 2. If you cannot use Form 940-EZ, you must use Form 940 instead.*

A   Enter the amount of contributions paid to your state unemployment fund. (See instructions for line A on page 4.) ▶ $ ....

B   (1) Enter the name of the state where you have to pay contributions   . . . . ▶   ....
        (2) Enter your state reporting number as shown on state unemployment tax return ▶

If you will not have to file returns in the future, check here (see **Who must file** on page 2) **and complete and sign the return** . . . . . ▶ ☐

If this is an Amended Return, check here . . . . ▶ ☐

Part I   Taxable Wages and FUTA Tax

1	Total payments (including payments shown on lines 2 and 3) during the calendar year for services of employees		**1**	
		Amount paid		
2	Exempt payments. (Explain all exempt payments, attaching additional sheets if necessary.) ▶	**2**		
3	Payments for services of more than $7,000. Enter only amounts over the first $7,000 paid to each employee. Do not include any exempt payments from line 2. Do not use your state wage limitation. The $7,000 amount is the Federal wage base. Your state wage base may be different	**3**		
4	Total exempt payments (add lines 2 and 3)		**4**	
5	**Total taxable wages** (subtract line 4 from line 1) . . . . ▶		**5**	
6	**FUTA tax.** Multiply the wages on line 5 by .008 and enter here. (If the result is over $100, also complete Part II.) .		**6**	
7	Total FUTA tax deposited for the year, including any overpayment applied from a prior year (from your records)		**7**	
8	**Amount you owe** (subtract line 7 from line 6). This should be $100 or less. Pay to "Internal Revenue Service." ▶		**8**	
9	**Overpayment** (subtract line 6 from line 7). Check if it is to be: ☐ **Applied to next return or** ☐ **Refunded** ▶		**9**	

Part II   Record of Quarterly Federal Unemployment Tax Liability (Do not include state liability.) Complete only if line 6 is over $100.

Quarter	First (Jan. 1 – Mar. 31)	Second (Apr. 1 – June 30)	Third (July 1 – Sept. 30)	Fourth (Oct. 1 – Dec. 31)	Total for year
Liability for quarter					

Under penalties of perjury, I declare that I have examined this return, including accompanying schedules and statements, and, to the best of my knowledge and belief, it is true, correct, and complete, and that no part of any payment made to a state unemployment fund claimed as a credit was, or is to be, deducted from the payments to employees.

MINI PRACTICE SET:
PETE'S MARKET

PETE'S MARKET
GENERAL JOURNAL

PAGE 6

Date		Account Titles and Description	PR			Dr.					Cr.			

MINI PRACTICE SET:
PETE'S MARKET

PETE'S MARKET
GENERAL JOURNAL

PAGE 7

Date		Account Titles and Description	PR		Dr.				Cr.		

MINI PRACTICE SET (CONTINUED):
PETE'S MARKET

PETE'S MARKET
GENERAL JOURNAL

PAGE 8

Date		Account Titles and Description	PR		Dr.				Cr.		

MINI PRACTICE SET (CONTINUED):
PETE'S MARKET

PETE'S MARKET
GENERAL JOURNAL

Date		Account Titles and Description	PR	Dr.	Cr.

Form 941
(Rev. January 199X)
Department of the Treasury
Internal Revenue Service   (O)

4141

Employer's Quarterly Federal Tax Return

▶ See separate instructions for information on completing this return.
Please type or print.

Enter state code for state in which deposits made . ▶ ☐ (see page 3 of instructions).

Name (as distinguished from trade name)	Date quarter ended
Trade name, if any	Employer identification number
Address (number and street)	City, state, and ZIP code

OMB No. 1545-0029

T	
FF	
FD	
FP	
I	
T	

If address is different from prior return, check here ▶ ☐

IRS Use

1 1 1 1 1 1 1 1 1 1	2	3 3 3 3 3 3	4 4 4

5 5 5   6   7   8 8 8 8 8 8   9 9 9   10 10 10 10 10 10 10 10 10

If you do not have to file returns in the future, check here ▶ ☐   and enter date final wages paid ▶

If you are a seasonal employer, see **Seasonal employers** on page 1 of the instructions and check here ▶ ☐

1	Number of employees (except household) employed in the pay period that includes March 12th ▶	**1**
2	Total wages and tips, plus other compensation	**2**
3	Total income tax withheld from wages, tips, and sick pay	**3**
4	Adjustment of withheld income tax for preceding quarters of calendar year	**4**
5	Adjusted total of income tax withheld (line 3 as adjusted by line 4—see instructions)	**5**
6	Taxable social security wages . . . . . 6a $ _____ × 12.4% (.124) =	**6b**
	Taxable social security tips . . . . . . 6c $ _____ × 12.4% (.124) =	**6d**
7	Taxable Medicare wages and tips . . . 7a $ _____ × 2.9% (.029) =	**7b**
8	Total social security and Medicare taxes (add lines 6b, 6d, and 7b). Check here if wages are not subject to social security and/or Medicare tax . . . . ▶ ☐	**8**
9	Adjustment of social security and Medicare taxes (see instructions for required explanation) Sick Pay $ _____ ± Fractions of Cents $ _____ ± Other $ _____ =	**9**
10	Adjusted total of social security and Medicare taxes (line 8 as adjusted by line 9—see instructions)	**10**
11	**Total taxes** (add lines 5 and 10)	**11**
12	Advance earned income credit (EIC) payments made to employees	**12**
13	Net taxes (subtract line 12 from line 11). **This should equal line 17, column (d) below** (or line D of Schedule B (Form 941))	**13**
14	Total deposits for quarter, including overpayment applied from a prior quarter	**14**
15	**Balance due** (subtract line 14 from line 13). See instructions	**15**

16 **Overpayment,** if line 14 is more than line 13, enter excess here ▶ $ _____
and check if to be: ☐ Applied to next return   **OR**   ☐ Refunded.

- **All filers:** If line 13 is less than $500, you need not complete line 17 or Schedule B.
- **Semiweekly schedule depositors:** Complete Schedule B and check here . . . . ▶ ☐
- **Monthly schedule depositors:** Complete line 17, columns (a) through (d), and check here . . . . . . ▶ ☐

17	**Monthly Summary of Federal Tax Liability**		
(a) First month liability	**(b)** Second month liability	**(c)** Third month liability	**(d)** Total liability for quarter

Sign Here

Under penalties of perjury, I declare that I have examined this return, including accompanying schedules and statements, and to the best of my knowledge and belief, it is true, correct, and complete.

Signature ▶ _____   Print Your Name and Title ▶ _____   Date ▶ _____

**COMPREHENSIVE REVIEW PROBLEM:
PETE'S MARKET**

Use the fold-out payroll register located at the end of this study guide.

FICA Social Security Payable	210
	410.90 (ee)
	410.90 (er)

FICA-Medicare Payable	212
	100 (ee)
	100 (er)

FIT Payable	220
	600

SIT Payable	225
	150

FUTA Tax Payable	230
	88

SUTA Payable	240
	155

SOLUTIONS TO ACCOUNTING RECALL

Part I

1.	H	**6.**	J
2.	D	**7.**	F
3.	E	**8.**	C
4.	A	**9.**	I
5.	G	**10.**	B

Part II

11. False

12. True

13. False; FIT and FICA (Social Security and Medicare) (ee + er)

14. False; More than $100 paid quarterly

15. True

SPECIAL JOURNALS: SALES AND CASH RECEIPTS

SELF-REVIEW QUIZ 9-1

1. _____ 2. _____ 3. _____ 4. _____ 5. _____

SELF-REVIEW QUIZ 9-2

1. _____ 2. _____ 3. _____ 4. _____ 5. _____ 6. _____ 7. _____ 8. _____

SELF-REVIEW QUIZ 9-3

MOSS COMPANY
SALES JOURNAL

PAGE 1

Date		Account Debited	Terms	Invoice No.	Post Ref.	Dr. Acc. Receivable Cr. Sales				

PAGE 1

Date	Account Titles and Description	PR	Dr.	Cr.

ACCOUNTS RECEIVABLE SUBSIDIARY LEDGER

NAME   JANE COMPANY

ADDRESS   118 MORRIS RD., BOSTON, MA 01935

Date	Explanation	Post Ref.	Debit	Credit	Dr. Balance

NAME   RALPH COMPANY

ADDRESS   31 NORRIS ROAD, BOSTON MA 01935

Date	Explanation	Post Ref.	Debit	Credit	Dr. Balance

PARTIAL GENERAL LEDGER

ACCOUNTS RECEIVABLE   ACCOUNT NO. 112

Date	Explanation	Post Ref.	Debit	Credit	Balance Debit	Balance Credit

SALES   ACCOUNT NO. 411

Date	Explanation	Post Ref.	Debit	Credit	Balance Debit	Balance Credit

SALES RETURNS AND ALLOWANCES   ACCOUNT NO. 412

Date	Explanation	Post Ref.	Debit	Credit	Balance Debit	Balance Credit

SELF-REVIEW QUIZ 9-4

MOORE COMPANY

CASH RECEIPTS JOURNAL

PAGE 2

Date	Cash Dr.	Sales Discounts Dr.	Accounts Receivable Cr.	Sales Cr.	Sundry		
					Account Name	Pr.	Amount Cr.

PARTIAL GENERAL LEDGER

CASH   ACCOUNT NO. 110

Date 19xx		Explanation	Post Ref.	Debit	Credit	Balance Debit	Balance Credit
May	1	Balance	✓			6 0 0 00	

ACCOUNTS RECEIVABLE   ACCOUNT NO. 120

Date 19xx		Explanation	Post Ref.	Debit	Credit	Balance Debit	Balance Credit
May	1	Balance	✓			7 0 0 00	

STORE EQUIPMENT   ACCOUNT NO. 130

Date 19xx		Explanation	Post Ref.	Debit	Credit	Balance Debit	Balance Credit
May	1	Balance	✓			6 0 0 00	

SALES   ACCOUNT NO. 410

Date 19xx		Explanation	Post Ref.	Debit	Credit	Balance Debit	Balance Credit
May	1	Balance	✓				7 0 0 00

SALES DISCOUNT   **ACCOUNT NO. 420**

Date 19xx		Explanation	Post Ref.	Debit	Credit	Balance Debit	Balance Credit

ACCOUNTS RECEIVABLE SUBSIDIARY LEDGER

NAME   IRENE WELCH

ADDRESS   10 RONG RD., BEVERLY, MA 01215

Date 19xx		Explanation	Post Ref.	Debit	Credit	Dr. Balance
May	1	Balance	✓			5 0 0 00

NAME   JANISS FROSS

ADDRESS   81 FOSTER RD., BEVERLY, MA 09125

Date 19xx		Explanation	Post Ref.	Debit	Credit	Dr. Balance
May	1	Balance	✓			2 0 0 00

FORMS FOR COMPREHENSIVE DEMONSTRATION PROBLEM

WALTER LANTZE CO.
GENERAL JOURNAL   PAGE 1

Date	Account Titles and Description	PR	Dr.	Cr.

WALTER LANTZE CO.
SALES JOURNAL
PAGE 1

Date	Account Debited	Terms	Invoice No.	Post Ref.	Dr. Acc. Receivable Cr. Sales

WALTER LANTZE CO.
CASH RECEIPTS JOURNAL   PAGE 1

Date	Cash Dr.	Sales Discounts Dr.	Accounts Receivable Cr.	Sales Cr.	Sundry Account Name	Pr.	Amount Cr.

PARTIAL GENERAL LEDGER

CASH   ACCOUNT NO. 111

Date	Explanation	Post Ref.	Debit	Credit	Balance Debit	Balance Credit

ACCOUNTS RECEIVABLE   ACCOUNT NO. 112

Date	Explanation	Post Ref.	Debit	Credit	Balance Debit	Balance Credit

WALTER LANTZ, CAPITAL   ACCOUNT NO. 311

Date	Explanation	Post Ref.	Debit	Credit	Balance Debit	Balance Credit

SALES   **ACCOUNT NO. 411**

Date	Explanation	Post Ref.	Debit	Credit	Balance Debit	Balance Credit

SALES RETURNS AND ALLOWANCES   **ACCOUNT NO. 412**

Date	Explanation	Post Ref.	Debit	Credit	Balance Debit	Balance Credit

SALES DISCOUNT   **ACCOUNT NO. 413**

Date	Explanation	Post Ref.	Debit	Credit	Balance Debit	Balance Credit

ACCOUNTS RECEIVABLE SUBSIDIARY LEDGER

NAME   **BUZZARD CO.**

ADDRESS   **1000 BURBANK AVE., CALIF 53210**

Date 19xx	Explanation	Post Ref.	Debit	Credit	Debit Balance

NAME   **PANDA CO.**

ADDRESS   **400 GRACIE AVE., LYNN, MA 019417**

Date 19xx	Explanation	Post Ref.	Debit	Credit	Debit Balance

LANTZE CO.
SCHEDULE OF ACCOUNTS RECEIVABLE
JULY 31, 19XX

YOU MAKE THE CALL: CRITICAL THINKING/ETHICAL CASE

CHAPTER 9
FORMS FOR MINI EXERCISES

1.

2.

3.

A._____ _____

B._____ _____

C._____ _____

4.

5.

A._____ _____

B._____ _____

C._____ _____

D._____ _____

BLUE CO.
SCHEDULE OF ACCOUNTS RECEIVABLE
MAY 31, 19XX

FORMS FOR EXERCISES

9-1.

Kevin Stone Co.	Accounts Receivable 112

Bill Valley Co.	Sales 412

9-2.

SALES JOURNAL

PAGE 1

Date		Account Debited	Terms	Invoice No.	Post Ref.	Dr. Accounts Receivable Cr. Sales		

Bass Co.	Sales 411

Ronald Co.	Accounts Receivable 112	Sales Returns & Allowances 412

GENERAL JOURNAL

PAGE 1

EXERCISES (CONTINUED)

9-3.

CASH RECEIPTS JOURNAL   **PAGE 1**

Date	Cash Dr.	Sales Discounts Dr.	Accounts Receivable Cr.	Sales Cr.	Sundry Account Names	Post Ref.	Amount Cr.

9-4.

SALES JOURNAL   **PAGE 1**

Date	Account Debited	Terms	Invoice No.	Post Ref.	Dr. Accounts Receivable Cr. Sales

CASH RECEIPTS JOURNAL   **PAGE 1**

Date	Cash Dr.	Sales Discounts Dr.	Accounts Receivable Cr.	Sales Cr.	Sundry Account Names	Post Ref.	Amount Cr.

EXERCISES (CONTINUED)

GENERAL JOURNAL

PAGE 1

Date	Account Titles and Description	PR	Dr.	Cr.

ACCOUNTS RECEIVABLE SUBSIDIARY LEDGER

PARTIAL GENERAL LEDGER

Boston Co.

Cash   111

Gary Co.

Accounts Receivable   113

Edna Cares, Capital   311

Sales   411

Sales Returns &
Allowances   412

Sales Discount   413

EDNA CO.
SCHEDULE OF ACCOUNTS RECEIVABLE
JUNE 30, 19XX

_____

_____

_____

_____

9-5. _____

_____

_____

_____

_____

END OF CHAPTER PROBLEMS

PROBLEM 9A-1 OR PROBLEM 9B-1

(1,2)

MAX COMPANY
SALES JOURNAL

PAGE 1

Date	Account Debited	Invoice No.	PR.	Accounts Receivable Dr.	Pizza Sales Cr.	Grocery Sales Cr.

(1,2)

MAX COMPANY
GENERAL JOURNAL

PAGE 1

Date	Account Titles and Description	PR	Dr.	Cr.

PROBLEM 9A-1 OR PROBLEM 9B-1 (CONTINUED)

ACCOUNTS RECEIVABLE SUBSIDIARY LEDGER

NAME   JOE KASE CO.

ADDRESS   942 MOSE ST., REVERE. MA 01938

Date	Explanation	Post Ref.	Debit	Credit	Dr. Balance

NAME   LONG CO.

ADDRESS   8 JOSS AVE., LYNN, MA 01947

Date	Explanation	Post Ref.	Debit	Credit	Dr. Balance

NAME   SUE MOORE CO.

ADDRESS   10 LOST RD., TOPSFIELD, MA 01998

Date	Explanation	Post Ref.	Debit	Credit	Dr. Balance

PROBLEM 9A-1 OR PROBLEM 9B-1 (CONTINUED)

MAX COMPANY
GENERAL LEDGER

ACCOUNTS RECEIVABLE   ACCOUNT NO. 112

Date	Explanation	Post Ref.	Debit	Credit	Balance Debit	Balance Credit

PIZZA SALES   ACCOUNT NO. 410

Date	Explanation	Post Ref.	Debit	Credit	Balance Debit	Balance Credit

GROCERY SALES   ACCOUNT NO. 411

Date	Explanation	Post Ref.	Debit	Credit	Balance Debit	Balance Credit

SALES RETURNS AND ALLOWANCES   ACCOUNT NO. 412

Date	Explanation	Post Ref.	Debit	Credit	Balance Debit	Balance Credit

PROBLEM 9A-1 OR PROBLEM 9B-1 (CONCLUDED)

MAX COMPANY
SCHEDULE OF ACCOUNTS RECEIVABLE
JUNE 30, 19XX

PROBLEM 9A-2 OR PROBLEM 9B-2

(1,2)

TED'S AUTO SUPPLY
SALES JOURNAL

PAGE 4

Date	Customer's Name Accounts Receivable	Invoice No.	PR.	Accounts Receivable Dr.	Sales Tax Payable Cr.	Auto Parts Sales Cr.

PROBLEM 9A-2 OR PROBLEM 9B-2 (CONTINUED)

(1,2)

TED'S AUTO SUPPLY
GENERAL JOURNAL

PAGE 2

Date		Account Titles and Description	PR	Dr.	Cr.

PROBLEM 9A-2 OR PROBLEM 9B-2 (CONTINUED)

ACCOUNTS RECEIVABLE SUBSIDIARY LEDGER

NAME LANCE CORNER

ADDRESS 9 ROE ST., BARTLETT, NH 01382

Date 19XX		Explanation	Post Ref.	Debit	Credit	Dr. Balance
NOV	1	Balance	√			4 0 0 00

NAME J. SETH

ADDRESS 22 REESE ST., LACONIA, NH 04321

Date 19XX		Explanation	Post Ref.	Debit	Credit	Dr. Balance
NOV	1	Balance	√			2 0 0 00

NAME R. VOLAN

ADDRESS 12 ASTER RD., MERIMACK, NH 02134

Date 19XX		Explanation	Post Ref.	Debit	Credit	Dr. Balance
NOV	1	Balance	√			1 0 0 0 00

PROBLEM 9A-2 OR PROBLEM 9B-2 (CONTINUED)

TED'S AUTO SUPPLY
PARTIAL GENERAL LEDGER

ACCOUNTS RECEIVABLE   **ACCOUNT NO. 110**

Date 19XX		Explanation	Post Ref.	Debit	Credit	Balance Debit	Balance Credit
NOV	1	Balance	√			1 6 0 0 00	

SALES TAX PAYABLE   **ACCOUNT NO. 210**

Date 19XX		Explanation	Post Ref.	Debit	Credit	Balance Debit	Balance Credit
NOV	1	Balance	√				1 6 0 0 00

AUTO PARTS SALES   **ACCOUNT NO. 410**

Date	Explanation	Post Ref.	Debit	Credit	Balance Debit	Balance Credit

SALES RETURNS AND ALLOWANCES   **ACCOUNT NO. 420**

Date	Explanation	Post Ref.	Debit	Credit	Balance Debit	Balance Credit

PROBLEM 9A-2 OR PROBLEM 9B-2 (CONCLUDED)

(3)

TED'S AUTO SUPPLY
SCHEDULE OF ACCOUNTS RECEIVABLE
NOVEMBER 30, 19XX

PROBLEM 9A-3 OR PROBLEM 9B-3
(1,2)

PEAKER'S SNEAKER SHOP
SALES JOURNAL

PAGE 5

Date		Customer's Name	Sales Ticket No.	Terms	PR.	Accounts Rec. - Dr. Sales - Cr.				

PROBLEM 9A-3 OR PROBLEM 9B-3 (CONTINUED)

PAGE 2

PEAKER'S SNEAKER SHOP
CASH RECEIPTS JOURNAL

Date	Cash Dr.	Sales Discounts Dr.	Accounts Receivable Cr.	Sales Cr.	Sundry Account Names	PR.	Amount Cr.

PROBLEM 9A-3 OR PROBLEM 9B-3 (CONTINUED)
(1,2)

PEAKER'S SNEAKER SHOP
GENERAL JOURNAL

PAGE 1

Date	Account Titles and Description	PR	Dr.	Cr.

ACCOUNTS RECEIVABLE SUBSIDIARY LEDGER

NAME   B. DALE

ADDRESS   1822 RIVER RD., MEMPHIS, TN 09111

Date 19XX		Explanation	Post Ref.	Debit	Credit	Dr. Balance
MAY	1	Balance	√			4 0 0 00

NAME   RON LESTER

ADDRESS   18 MASS. AVE., SAN DIEGO, CA 01999

Date 19XX		Explanation	Post Ref.	Debit	Credit	Dr. Balance
MAY	1	Balance	√			8 0 0 00

PROBLEM 9A-3 OR PROBLEM 9B-3 (CONTINUED)

ACCOUNTS RECEIVABLE SUBSIDIARY LEDGER

NAME   PAM PRY

ADDRESS   918 MOORE DRD., HOMEWOOD, IL 60430

Date 19XX	Explanation	Post Ref.	Debit	Credit	Dr. Balance
MAY 1	Balance	√			600 00

NAME   JIM ZON

ADDRESS   2 CHESTNUT ST., SWAMPSCOTT, MA 01970

Date 19XX	Explanation	Post Ref.	Debit	Credit	Dr. Balance
May 1	Balance	√			400 00

PEAKER'S SNEAKER SHOP
PARTIAL GENERAL LEDGER

CASH   ACCOUNT NO. 10

Date 19XX	Explanation	Post Ref.	Debit	Credit	Balance Debit	Balance Credit
MAY 1	Balance	√			15 500 00	

PROBLEM 9A-3 OR PROBLEM 9B-3 (CONTINUED)

ACCOUNTS RECEIVABLE — ACCOUNT NO. 12

Date 19XX		Explanation	Post Ref.	Debit	Credit	Balance Debit	Balance Credit
MAY	1	Balance	√			2 2 0 0 00	

SNEAKER RACK EQUIPMENT — ACCOUNT NO. 14

Date 19XX		Explanation	Post Ref.	Debit	Credit	Balance Debit	Balance Credit
MAY	1	Balance	√			1 0 0 0 00	

MARK PEAKER, CAPITAL — ACCOUNT NO. 30

Date 19XX		Explanation	Post Ref.	Debit	Credit	Balance Debit	Balance Credit
MAY	1	Balance	√				40 0 0 0 00

SALES — ACCOUNT NO. 40

Date 19XX		Explanation	Post Ref.	Debit	Credit	Balance Debit	Balance Credit
MAY	1	Balance	√				2 2 0 0 00

PROBLEM 9A-3 OR PROBLEM 9B-3 (CONCLUDED)

SALES DISCOUNT   ACCOUNT NO. _42_

Date 19XX	Explanation	Post Ref.	Debit	Credit	Balance Debit	Balance Credit

SALES RETURNS & ALLOWANCES   ACCOUNT NO. _44_

Date 19XX	Explanation	Post Ref.	Debit	Credit	Balance Debit	Balance Credit

(3)

PEAKER'S SNEAKER SHOP
SCHEDULE OF ACCOUNTS RECEIVABLE
MAY 31, 19XX

PROBLEM 9A-4 OR PROBLEM 9B-4

BILL'S COSMETIC MARKET
SALES JOURNAL

PAGE 1

Date	Customer	Sales Ticket	PR.	Accounts Receivable Dr.	Sales Tax Payable Cr.	Lipstick Sales Cr.	Eyeshadow Sales Cr.

PROBLEM 9A-4 OR PROBLEM 9B-4 (CONTINUED)

BILL'S COSMETIC MARKET
CASH RECEIPTS JOURNAL

PAGE 1

Date	Cash Dr.	Accounts Receivable Cr.	Sales Tax Payable Cr.	Lipstick Sales Cr.	Eyeshadow Sales Cr.	Sundry		
						Account Names	PR.	Amount Cr.

PROBLEM 9A-4 OR PROBLEM 9B-4 (CONTINUED)

(1,2)

BILL'S COSMETIC MARKET
GENERAL JOURNAL

PAGE 1

Date		Account Titles and Description	PR		Dr.		Cr.

ACCOUNTS RECEIVABLE SUBSIDIARY LEDGER

NAME ALICE KOY CO.

ADDRESS 2 RYAN RD., BUFFALO, NY 09113

Date		Explanation	Post Ref.	Debit		Credit		Debit Balance

PROBLEM 9A-4 OR PROBLEM 9B-4 (CONTINUED)

ACCOUNTS RECEIVABLE SUBSIDIARY LEDGER

NAME   RUSTY NEAL CO.

ADDRESS   4 REEL RD., LANCASTER, PA 04332

Date	Explanation	Post Ref.	Debit	Credit	Debit Balance

NAME   MARIKA SANCHEZ CO.

ADDRESS   14 BONE DR., ENGLEWOOD CLIFFS, NJ 07632

Date	Explanation	Post Ref.	Debit	Credit	Debit Balance

NAME   JEFF TONG CO.

ADDRESS   2 MARION RD. , BOSTON, MA 01981

Date	Explanation	Post Ref.	Debit	Credit	Debit Balance

PROBLEM 9A-4 OR PROBLEM 9B-4 (CONTINUED)

BILL'S COSMETIC MARKET
PARTIAL GENERAL LEDGER

CASH   ACCOUNT NO. __10__

Date	Explanation	Post Ref.	Debit	Credit	Balance Debit	Balance Credit

ACCOUNTS RECEIVABLE   ACCOUNT NO. __12__

Date	Explanation	Post Ref.	Debit	Credit	Balance Debit	Balance Credit

SALES TAX PAYABLE   ACCOUNT NO. __20__

Date	Explanation	Post Ref.	Debit	Credit	Balance Debit	Balance Credit

BILL MURRAY, CAPITAL   ACCOUNT NO. __30__

Date	Explanation	Post Ref.	Debit	Credit	Balance Debit	Balance Credit

PROBLEM 9A-4 OR PROBLEM 9B-4 (CONTINUED)

LIPSTICK SALES ACCOUNT NO. __40__

Date	Explanation	Post Ref.	Debit	Credit	Balance Debit	Balance Credit

SALES RETURNS AND ALLOWANCES, LIPSTICK ACCOUNT NO. __42__

Date	Explanation	Post Ref.	Debit	Credit	Balance Debit	Balance Credit

EYESHADOW SALES ACCOUNT NO. __44__

Date	Explanation	Post Ref.	Debit	Credit	Balance Debit	Balance Credit

PROBLEM 9A-4 (CONCLUDED)

(3)

BILL'S COSMETIC MARKET
SCHEDULE OF ACCOUNTS RECEIVABLE
APRIL 30, 19XX

CHAPTER 9
SUMMARY PRACTICE TEST
SPECIAL JOURNALS: SALES AND
CASH RECEIPTS

Part I Instructions

Fill in the blank(s) to complete the statement.

1. The normal balance of Sales Discounts is _____.
2. _____ _____ and _____ is a contra-revenue account.
3. Sales discount is a _____ account.
4. A discount period is less time than the _____ _____.
5. A _____ _____ records the sale of merchandise on account.
6. The _____ _____ _____ _____ lists in alphabetical order an account for each customer.
7. _____ _____ in the general ledger is called the controlling account.
8. The (√) in the sales journal indicates that the accounts receivable ledger has been updated _____ _____ _____.
9. The totals of the sales journal are posted at _____ _____ _____ _____ to the general ledger account.
10. In a wholesale company there is no _____ tax.
11. Sales Tax Payable is a _____ in the general ledger.
12. Issuing a _____ -_____ results in the seller reducing its accounts receivable.
13. Sales Returns and Allowances is a _____ account.
14. The _____ _____ _____ records the receipt of cash from any source.
15. The total of the _____ column in the cash receipts journal is never posted.
16. _____ is a process that helps prove the accuracy of recording transactions in the cash receipts journal.
17. No _____ _____ are taken on sales tax.
18. A _____ _____ _____ _____ lists the ending balances from the accounts receivable ledger.

Part II Instructions

From the following chart, complete the statements below.

CASH RECEIPTS JOURNAL

Cash Dr.				Sales Discounts Dr.				Accounts Receivable Cr.				Sales Cr.				Sundry Account Cr.			
		X	XX (F)											X	XX (I)				
					X	XX (G)			X	XX (H)			X	XX			X	XX (J)
					X	XX			X	XX			X	XX				
		X	XX (E)		X	XX (D)			X	XX (C)			X	XX (B)			X	XX (A)

1. **EXAMPLE:** *A is never posted.*

2. B is posted at _____ _____
_____ to the Sales account in the general ledger.

3. C is posted to _____ _____, the controlling account
in the general ledger at the end of the month.

4. D has a _____ balance that is posted to Sales Discount in the
general ledger at the end of the month.

5. E is posted _____ _____
_____ to the Cash account in the general ledger.

6. F should _____ _____ _____,
because the total will be posted to the Cash account in the
genneral ledger at the end of the month.

7. G is _____ _____ during the month.

8. H is _____ recorded to the accounts receivable subsidiary ledger during the
month.

9. I is _____ _____ during the month, because the total
of the Sales column is posted at the end of the month to Sales in the general
ledger.

10. J is posted to the _____ _____ during the month,
as the total of sundry is never posted.

Part III Instructions

Answer true or false to the following statements.

1. A schedule of accounts receivable is prepared from the general ledger.

2. Cross-footing verifies the accuracy of recording transactions into special journals.

3. (X) means the accounts receivable ledger has been updated.

4. The total of the sundry column is posted at the end of the month.

5. The cash receipts journal records sales on account.

6. Issuing a credit memorandum results in Sales, Returns and Allowances decreasing with Accounts Receivable increasing.

7. A (Đ) means the total of sundry is posted daily.

8. The sum of the accounts receivable subsidiary ledger is equal to the balance in the controlling account at the end of the month.

9. The sales journal records cash sales.

10. The accounts receivable subsidiary ledger is listed in numerical order .

11. Sales Returns and Allowances is a contra-revenue account.

12. Net sales = gross sales – SRA-SD.

13. All businesses must have a sales journal to record cash sales.

14. Discounts are taken on sales tax.

15. The total of the Sales Tax Payable is posted at the end of the month to the accounts receivable subsidiary ledger.

16. The accounts receivable subsidiary ledger is always located in the general ledger.

17. Gross profit plus operating expenses equals net income.

18. A credit period is longer than the discount period.

19. In the accounts receivable subsidiary ledger each account is debited to record amounts customers owe.

20. Special journals reduce posting labor.

CHAPTER 9
SOLUTIONS TO SUMMARY PRACTICE TEST

Part I

1. Debit
2. Sales Returns and Allowances
3. contra-revenue
4. credit period
5. sales journal
6. accounts receivable subsidiary ledger
7. Accounts Receivable
8. during the month
9. end of the month

10. sales
11. liability
12. credit memorandum
13. contra-revenue
14. cash receipts journal
15. sundry
16. cross-footing
17. cash discounts
18. schedule of accounts receivable

Part II

1. never posted
2. end of month
3. Accounts Receivable
4. debit
5. end of month
6. not be posted
7. not posted
8. immediately
9. not posted
10. general ledger

Part III

1. false
2. true
3. false
4. false
5. false
6. false
7. false
8. true
9. false
10. false

11. true
12. true
13. false
14. false
15. false
16. false
17. false
18. true
19. true
20. true

CHAPTERS 1-9
ACCOUNTING RECALL FORMS

Part I   **Part II**

1. _____   6. _____   11. _____
2. _____   7. _____   12. _____
3. _____   8. _____   13. _____
4. _____   9. _____   14. _____
5. _____   10. _____   15. _____

CONTINUING PROBLEM FOR CHAPTER 9

SALES JOURNAL   PAGE 1

Date	Account Debited	Terms	Invoice No.	Post Ref.	Dr. Accounts Receivable Cr. Sales

CASH RECEIPTS JOURNAL   PAGE 1

Date	Cash Dr.	Sales Discounts Dr.	Accounts Receivable Cr.	Sales Cr.	Sundry Account Names	Post Ref.	Amount Cr.

GENERAL JOURNAL   PAGE 10

Date	Account Titles and Description	PR	Dr.	Cr.

ELDORADO COMPUTER CENTER
SCHEDULE OF ACCOUNTS RECEIVABLE
1/31/XX

CASH   **ACCOUNT NO. 1000**

Date		Explanation	Post Ref.	Debit	Credit	Balance Debit	Balance Credit
1/1	XX	Balance forward	√			3 3 3 6 65	

ELDORADO COMPUTER CENTER
PARTIAL GENERAL LEDGER

ACCOUNTS RECEIVABLE   **ACCOUNT NO. 1020**

Date		Explanation	Post Ref.	Debit	Credit	Balance Debit	Balance Credit
1/1	XX	Balance forward				13 600 00	

SALES   **ACCOUNT NO.**

Date		Explanation	Post Ref.	Debit	Credit	Balance Debit	Balance Credit

SALES RETURN AND ALLOWANCES   **ACCOUNT NO. 4020**

Date		Explanation	Post Ref.	Debit	Credit	Balance Debit	Balance Credit

SALES DISCOUNTS   **ACCOUNT NO. 4030**

Date		Explanation	Post Ref.	Debit	Credit	Balance Debit	Balance Credit

NAME   TAYLOR GOLF   **ACCOUNT NO. 100**
ADDRESS   1010 MOCKINGBIRD LANE, CARLSBAD, CA 92008

Date		Explanation	Post Ref.	Debit	Credit	Dr. Balance
1/1	XX	Balance forward	√			2 9 0 0 00

NAME   VITA NEEDLE   **ACCOUNT NO. 101**
ADDRESS   144 CANTATA, IRVINE, CA 92606

Date		Explanation	Post Ref.	Debit	Credit	Dr. Balance
1/1	XX	Balance forward	√			6 8 0 0 00

NAME   ACCUPAC   **ACCOUNT NO. 103**
ADDRESS   1717 JORDAN ST., SAN CLEMENTE, CA 91607

Date		Explanation	Post Ref.	Debit	Credit	Dr. Balance
1/1	XX	Balance forward	√			3 9 0 0 00

ACCOUNTS RECEIVABLE SUBSIDIARY LEDGER

NAME   ANTHONY J. PITALE   **ACCOUNT NO. 104**

ADDRESS   600 NEWPORT BEACH, NEWPORT, CA 91600

Date	Explanation	Post Ref.	Debit	Credit	Dr. Balance

SOLUTIONS TO ACCOUNTING RECALL

Part I

1. E		**6.** C	
2. F		**7.** J	
3. H		**8.** B	
4. D		**9.** G	
5. I		**10.** A	

Part II

11. False; Ending Inventory

12. True

13. False; (SRA is increasing

14. True

15. False; (Subsidiary Account has been updated)

SPECIAL JOURNALS: PURCHASES AND CASH PAYMENTS

SELF-REVIEW QUIZ 10-1

1. _____ 2. _____ 3. _____ 4. _____ 5. _____

SELF-REVIEW QUIZ 10-2

MUNROE CO.
PURCHASES JOURNAL

PAGE 2

Date	Account Credited	Date of Invoice	Inv. No.	Terms	PR	Accounts Payable Cr.	Purchases Dr.	Sundry Dr.		
								Account	PR	Amount

MUNROE CO.
GENERAL JOURNAL

Date	Account Titles and Description	PR	Dr.	Cr.

ACCOUNTS PAYABLE SUBSIDIARY LEDGER

NAME   **JOHN BUTLER COMPANY**

ADDRESS   **18 REED RD., HOMEWOOD, IL 60430**

Date	Explanation	Post Ref.	Debit	Credit	Cr. Balance

NAME   **FLYNN COMPANY**

ADDRESS   **15 FOSS AVE., ENGLEWOD CLIFFS, NJ 07632**

Date	Explanation	Post Ref.	Debit	Credit	Cr. Balance

PARTIAL GENERAL LEDGER

EQUIPMENT   **ACCOUNT NO. 121**

Date	Explanation	Post Ref.	Debit	Credit	Balance Debit	Balance Credit

ACCOUNTS PAYABLE   ACCOUNT NO. 212

Date	Explanation	Post Ref.	Debit	Credit	Balance Debit	Balance Credit

PURCHASES   ACCOUNT NO. 512

Date	Explanation	Post Ref.	Debit	Credit	Balance Debit	Balance Credit

PURCHASES RETURNS AND ALLOWANCES   ACCOUNT NO. 513

Date	Explanation	Post Ref.	Debit	Credit	Balance Debit	Balance Credit

SELF-REVIEW QUIZ 10-3

MELISSA COMPANY
CASH PAYMENTS JOURNAL   PAGE 2

Date	Check No.	Accounts Debited	PR.	Sundry Account Dr.	Accounts Payable Dr.	Purchases Discounts Cr.	Cash Cr.

ACCOUNTS PAYABLE SUBSIDIARY LEDGER

NAME   **BOB FINKELSTEIN**

ADDRESS   **112 FLYING HIGHWAY, TRENTON, NJ 03111**

Date 19xx		Explanation	Post Ref.	Debit	Credit	Cr. Balance
June	1	Balance	√			3 0 0 00

NAME   **AL JEEP**

ADDRESS   **118 WANG RD., SAUGUS, MA 01432**

Date 19xx		Explanation	Post Ref.	Debit	Credit	Cr. Balance
June	1	Balance	√			2 0 0 00

PARTIAL GENERAL LEDGER

CASH   **ACCOUNT NO. 110**

Date 19XX		Explanation	Post Ref.	Debit	Credit	Balance Debit	Balance Credit
June	1	Balance	√			7 0 0 00	

ACCOUNTS PAYABLE   **ACCOUNT NO. 210**

Date 19XX		Explanation	Post Ref.	Debit	Credit	Balance Debit	Balance Credit
June	1	Balance	√				5 0 0 00

PURCHASES DISCOUNT   ACCOUNT NO. 511

Date		Explanation	Post Ref.	Debit	Credit	Balance	
						Debit	Credit

ADVERTISING EXPENSE   ACCOUNT NO. 610

Date		Explanation	Post Ref.	Debit	Credit	Balance	
						Debit	Credit

FORMS FOR COMPREHENSIVE DEMONSTRATION PROBLEM

J. LING CO.
SALES JOURNAL

PAGE 1

Date	Account Debited	Terms	Invoice No.	Post Ref.	Dr. Acc. Receivable Cr. Sales

CASH RECEIPTS JOURNAL

PAGE 1

Date	Cash Dr.	Sales Discounts Dr.	Accounts Receivable Cr.	Sales Cr.	Sundry		
					Account Name	Pr.	Amount Cr.

PURCHASES JOURNAL

PAGE 1

Date	Account Credited	Terms	PR	Accounts Payable Cr.	Purchases Dr.	Sundry Dr.		
						Account	PR	Amount

CASH PAYMENT JOURNAL

PAGE 1

Date	Check No.	Accounts Debited	PR.	Sundry Account Dr.	Accounts Payable Dr.	Purchases Discounts Cr.	Cash Cr.

GENERAL JOURNAL

PAGE 1

Date	Account Titles and Description	PR	Dr.	Cr.

ACCOUNTS RECEIVABLE SUBSIDIARY LEDGER

NAME BALDER CO.

ADDRESS 1 ROCK RD., DENVER, CO 66083

Date	Explanation	Post Ref.	Debit	Credit	Dr. Balance

NAME LEWIS CO.

ADDRESS 15 SMITH AVE., REVERE, MA 01545

Date	Explanation	Post Ref.	Debit	Credit	Dr. Balance

ACCOUNTS PAYABLE SUBSIDIARY LEDGER

NAME   **CASE CO.**

ADDRESS   **1 LONG RD., MARLEBORO, MA 01545**

Date	Explanation	Post Ref.	Debit	Credit	Cr. Balance

NAME   **NOONE CO.**

ADDRESS   **11 MILL RD., MALDEN, OK 01143**

Date	Explanation	Post Ref.	Debit	Credit	Cr. Balance

PARTIAL GENERAL LEDGER

Cash	111	Sales	410	Purchases Discounts	530

Accounts Receivable	112	Sales Returns & Allowances	420	Salaries Expense	610

Equipment	116	Sales Discount	430

Accounts Payable	210	Purchases	510

J. Ling, Capital	310	Purchases Returns & Allowances	520

YOU MAKE THE CALL: CRITICAL THINKING/ETHICAL CASE

_____

_____

_____

_____

_____

_____

_____

_____

_____

_____

_____

_____

_____

_____

_____

_____

_____

_____

_____

_____

_____

_____

_____

_____

_____

_____

_____

_____

_____

_____

_____

_____

_____

_____

_____

_____

_____

_____

_____

_____

_____

CHAPTER 10
FORMS FOR MINI EXERCISES

1. A. _____

   B. _____

   C. _____

   D. _____

   E. _____

   F. _____

   G. _____

   H. _____

2.

3.

_____

_____

_____

_____

_____

_____

_____

_____

_____

_____

4. A. _____   _____   5. A. _____   E. _____

   B. _____   _____   B. _____   F. _____

   C. _____   _____   C. _____

                                         D. _____

6.

AVE. CO
SCHEDULE OF ACCOUNTS PAYABLE
MAY 31, 19XX

FORMS FOR EXERCISES

10-1.

Barr Co.		Equipment 120

Jess Co.		Accounts Payable 210

Rey Co.		Purchases 510

10-2.   PAGE 1

Reel Co.		Accounts Payable 211		Purchases Returns and Allowances 513

Name_____ Class _____ Date _____

FORMS FOR EXERCISES (CONTINUED)

10-3.

PAGE 2

Date	Check No.	Accounts Debited	PR.	Sundry Account Dr.	Accounts Payable Dr.	Purchases Discount Cr.	Cash Cr.

ACCOUNTS PAYABLE SUBSIDIARY LEDGER

A. James
| | 1,000 |

B. Foss
| | 400 |

J. Ranch
| | 900 |

B. Swanson
| | 100 |

PARTIAL GENERAL LEDGER

Cash   110
| 3,000 | |

Accounts Payable   210
| | 2,400 |

Purchases Discount 511

Advertising Expense 610

EXERCISES (CONTINUED)

10-4.

MORGAN'S CLOTHING
SCHEDULE OF ACCOUNTS PAYABLE
APRIL 30, 19XX

Accounts Payable 210

10-5.

Accounts Affected	Category	Rules

10-6.

END OF CHAPTER PROBLEMS

PROBLEM 10A-1 OR PROBLEM 10B-1

PAGE 3

CLARK'S SPORTING GOODS SHOP
PURCHASES JOURNAL

Date	Account Credited	Date of Invoice	Inv. No.	Terms	PR	Accounts Payable Cr.	Purchases Dr.	Sundry Dr.		
								Account	PR	Amount

PROBLEM 10A-1 OR PROBLEM 10B-1 (CONTINUED)

ACCOUNTS PAYABLE SUBSIDIARY LEDGER

NAME   ASTER CO.

ADDRESS   12 SMITH ST., DEARBORN, MI 09113

Date	Explanation	Post Ref.	Debit	Credit	Cr. Balance

NAME   NORTON CO.

ADDRESS   1 RANTOUL RD., CHARLOTTE, NC 01114

Date	Explanation	Post Ref.	Debit	Credit	Cr. Balance

NAME   ROLO CO.

ADDRESS   2 WEST RD., LYNN, MA 01471

Date	Explanation	Post Ref.	Debit	Credit	Cr. Balance

PARTIAL GENERAL LEDGER

STORE SUPPLIES   ACCOUNT NO. __115__

Date	Explanation	Post Ref.	Debit	Credit	Balance Debit	Balance Credit

PROBLEM 10A-1 OR PROBLEM 10B-1 (CONCLUDED)

STORE EQUIPMENT   ACCOUNT NO. _121_

Date	Explanation	Post Ref.	Debit	Credit	Balance Debit	Balance Credit

ACCOUNTS PAYABLE   ACCOUNT NO. _210_

Date	Explanation	Post Ref.	Debit	Credit	Balance Debit	Balance Credit

PURCHASES   ACCOUNT NO. _510_

Date	Explanation	Post Ref.	Debit	Credit	Balance Debit	Balance Credit

PROBLEM 10A-2 OR PROBLEM 10B-2

PAGE 10

MABEL'S NATURAL FOOD STORE
PURCHASES JOURNAL

| Date | Account Credited | Date of Invoice | Inv. No. | Terms | PR | Accounts Payable Cr. | Purchases Dr. | Store Supplies Dr. | Sundry Dr. | | |
									Account	PR	Amount

PROBLEM 10A-2 OR PROBLEM 10B-2 (CONTINUED)

ACCOUNTS PAYABLE SUBSIDIARY LEDGER

NAME ATON CO.

ADDRESS 11 LYNNWAY AVE., NEWPORT, RI 03112

Date 19XX		Explanation	Post Ref.	Debit	Credit	Cr. Balance
MAY	1	Balance	√			4 0 0 00

NAME BROWARD CO.

ADDRESS 21 RIVER ST., ANAHEIM, CA 43110

Date 19XX		Explanation	Post Ref.	Debit	Credit	Cr. Balance
MAY	1	Balance	√			6 0 0 00

NAME MIDDEN CO.

ADDRESS 10 ASTER RD., DUBUQUE, IA 80021

Date 19XX		Explanation	Post Ref.	Debit	Credit	Cr. Balance
MAY	1	Balance	√			1 2 0 0 00

NAME RELAR CO.

ADDRESS 22 GERALD RD., SMITH, CO 43138

Date 19XX		Explanation	Post Ref.	Debit	Credit	Cr. Balance
MAY	1	Balance	√			5 0 0 00

PROBLEM 10A-2 OR PROBLEM 10B-2 (CONTINUED)

PARTIAL GENERAL LEDGER

STORE SUPPLIES ACCOUNT NO. 110

Date	Explanation	Post Ref.	Debit	Credit	Balance Debit	Balance Credit

OFFICE EQUIPMENT ACCOUNT NO. 120

Date	Explanation	Post Ref.	Debit	Credit	Balance Debit	Balance Credit

ACCOUNTS PAYABLE ACCOUNT NO. 210

Date 19XX	Explanation	Post Ref.	Debit	Credit	Balance Debit	Balance Credit
May 1	Balance	√				2 7 0 0 00

PURCHASES ACCOUNT NO. 510

Date 19XX	Explanation	Post Ref.	Debit	Credit	Balance Debit	Balance Credit
May 1	Balance	√			16 0 0 0 00	

PROBLEM 10A-2 OR PROBLEM 10B-2 (CONCLUDED)

PURCHASES RETURNS AND ALLOWANCES   ACCOUNT NO.   512

Date 19XX	Explanation	Post Ref.	Debit	Credit	Balance Debit	Balance Credit

GENERAL JOURNAL

PAGE 2

Date	Account Titles and Description	PR	Dr.	Cr.

MABEL'S NATURAL FOOD STORE
SCHEDULE OF ACCOUNTS PAYABLE
MAY 31, 19XX

PROBLEM 10A-3 OR PROBLEM 10B-3

(1,2)

JONES' COMPUTER CENTER
CASH PAYMENTS JOURNAL

PAGE 5

Date	Check No.	Account Debited	PR.	Sundry Dr.	Accounts Payable Dr.	Computer Purchases Dr.	Computer Purchases Discount Cr.	Cash Cr.

PROBLEM 10A-3 OR PROBLEM 10B-3
ACCOUNTS PAYABLE SUBSIDIARY LEDGER

NAME   ALVIN CO.

ADDRESS   1 REACH RD., IPSWICH, MA 01932

Date 19XX		Explanation	Post Ref.	Debit	Credit	Cr. Balance
MAY	1	Balance	√			1 2 0 0 00

NAME   HENRY CO.

ADDRESS   1 RALPH RD., REVERE, MA 01321

Date 19XX		Explanation	Post Ref.	Debit	Credit	Cr. Balance
MAY	1	Balance	√			6 0 0 00

NAME   SOY CO.

ADDRESS   7 PLYMOUTH AVE., GLENN, NH 01218

Date 19XX		Explanation	Post Ref.	Debit	Credit	Cr. Balance
MAY	1	Balance	√			8 0 0 00

NAME   XON CO.

ADDRESS   22 REY RD., BOCA RATON, FL 99132

Date 19XX		Explanation	Post Ref.	Debit	Credit	Cr. Balance
MAY	1	Balance	√			1 4 0 0 00

PROBLEM 10A-3 OR PROBLEM 10B-3 (CONTINUED)

PARTIAL GENERAL LEDGER

CASH — ACCOUNT NO. 110

Date 19XX		Explanation	Post Ref.	Debit	Credit	Balance Debit	Balance Credit
May	1	Balance	√			17 0 0 0 00	

DELIVERY TRUCK — ACCOUNT NO. 150

Date		Explanation	Post Ref.	Debit	Credit	Balance Debit	Balance Credit

ACCOUNTS PAYABLE — ACCOUNT NO. 210

Date 19XX		Explanation	Post Ref.	Debit	Credit	Balance Debit	Balance Credit
May	1	Balance	√				4 0 0 0 00

COMPUTER PURCHASES — ACCOUNT NO. 510

Date 19XX		Explanation	Post Ref.	Debit	Credit	Balance Debit	Balance Credit

PROBLEM 10A-3 OR PROBLEM 10B-3 (CONCLUDED)

COMPUTER PURCHASES DISCOUNT   **ACCOUNT NO. __511__**

Date	Explanation	Post Ref.	Debit	Credit	Balance Debit	Balance Credit

RENT EXPENSE   **ACCOUNT NO. __610__**

Date	Explanation	Post Ref.	Debit	Credit	Balance Debit	Balance Credit

UTILITIES EXPENSE   **ACCOUNT NO. __620__**

Date	Explanation	Post Ref.	Debit	Credit	Balance Debit	Balance Credit

JONES, COMPUTER CENTER
SCHEDULE OF ACCOUNTS PAYABLE
MAY 31, 19XX

PROBLEM 10A-4 OR PROBLEM 10B-4
(1,2,3)

PAGE 1

ABBY'S TOY HOUSE
PURCHASES JOURNAL

Date	Account Credited	Date of Inv.	Inv. No.	Terms	PR	Accounts Payable Cr.	Toy Purchases Dr.	Sundry Dr.		
								Accounts	PR	Amount

PROBLEM 10A-4 OR PROBLEM 10B-4 (CONTINUED)

ABBY'S TOY HOUSE
CASH RECEIPTS JOURNAL

PAGE 1

Date	Cash Dr.	Sales Discounts Dr.	Accounts Receivable Cr.	Toy Sales Cr.	Sundry Account	Pr.	Amount Cr.

ABBY'S TOY HOUSE
CASH PAYMENTS JOURNAL

PAGE 1

Date	Check No.	Account Debited	PR.	Sundry Dr.	Accounts Payable Dr.	Purchases Discount Cr.	Cash Cr.

PROBLEM 10A-4 OR PROBLEM 10B-4 (CONTINUED)

ABBY'S TOY HOUSE
SALES JOURNAL

PAGE 1

Date	Account Debited	Invoice No.	Terms	PR.	Accounts Rec. - Dr. Toy Sales - Cr.

ABBY'S TOY HOUSE
GENERAL JOURNAL

PAGE 1

Date	Account Titles and Description	PR	Dr.	Cr.

PROBLEM 10A-4 OR PROBLEM 10B-4 (CONTINUED)

(4)

ABBY'S TOY HOUSE
SCHEDULE OF ACCOUNTS RECEIVABLE
MARCH 31, 19XX

(4)

ABBY'S TOY HOUSE
SCHEDULE OF ACCOUNTS PAYABLE
MARCH 31, 19XX

PROBLEM 10A-4 OR PROBLEM 10B-4 (CONTINUED)

ACCOUNTS PAYABLE SUBSIDIARY LEDGER

NAME   MINNIE KATZ

ADDRESS   87 GARFIELD AVE., REVERE, MA 01245

Date	Explanation	Post Ref.	Debit	Credit	Cr. Balance

NAME   SAM KATZ GARAGE

ADDRESS   22 REGIS RD., BOSTON, MA 01950

Date	Explanation	Post Ref.	Debit	Credit	Cr. Balance

NAME   EARL MILLER CO.

ADDRESS   22 RETTER ST., SAN DIEGO, CA 01211

Date	Explanation	Post Ref.	Debit	Credit	Cr. Balance

NAME   WOODY SMITH

ADDRESS   2 SPRING ST., WEERS, ND 02118

Date	Explanation	Post Ref.	Debit	Credit	Cr. Balance

PROBLEM 10A-4 OR PROBLEM 10B-4 (CONTINUED)

ACCOUNTS RECEIVABLE SUBSIDIARY LEDGER

NAME   BILL BURTON

ADDRESS   24 RYAN RD., BUIKE, OH 02183

Date	Explanation	Post Ref.	Debit	Credit	Dr. Balance

NAME   BONNIE FLOW CO.

ADDRESS   2 SMITH RD., DALLAS, TX 22210

Date	Explanation	Post Ref.	Debit	Credit	Dr. Balance

NAME   JIM REX

ADDRESS   1 SCHOOL ST., CLEVELAND, OH 22441

Date	Explanation	Post Ref.	Debit	Credit	Dr. Balance

PROBLEM 10A-4 OR PROBLEM 10B-4 (CONTINUED)

NAME   AMY ROSE

ADDRESS   18 VEEK RD., CHESTER, CT 80111

Date	Explanation	Post Ref.	Debit	Credit	Dr. Balance

GENERAL LEDGER

CASH   ACCOUNT NO. __110__

Date	Explanation	Post Ref.	Debit	Credit	Balance Debit	Balance Credit

ACCOUNTS RECEIVABLE   ACCOUNT NO. __112__

Date	Explanation	Post Ref.	Debit	Credit	Balance Debit	Balance Credit

PREPAID RENT   ACCOUNT NO. __114__

Date	Explanation	Post Ref.	Debit	Credit	Balance Debit	Balance Credit

PROBLEM 10A-4 OR PROBLEM 10B-4 (CONTINUED)

DELIVERY TRUCK   ACCOUNT NO. _121_

Date	Explanation	Post Ref.	Debit	Credit	Balance Debit	Balance Credit

ACCOUNTS PAYABLE   ACCOUNT NO. _210_

Date	Explanation	Post Ref.	Debit	Credit	Balance Debit	Balance Credit

A. ELLEN, CAPITAL   ACCOUNT NO. _310_

Date	Explanation	Post Ref.	Debit	Credit	Balance Debit	Balance Credit

TOY SALES   ACCOUNT NO. _410_

Date	Explanation	Post Ref.	Debit	Credit	Balance Debit	Balance Credit

PROBLEM 10A-4 OR PROBLEM 10B-4 (CONTINUED)

SALES RETURNS AND ALLOWANCES   ACCOUNT NO. __412__

Date	Explanation	Post Ref.	Debit	Credit	Balance Debit	Balance Credit

SALES DISCOUNTS   ACCOUNT NO. __414__

Date	Explanation	Post Ref.	Debit	Credit	Balance Debit	Balance Credit

TOY PURCHASES   ACCOUNT NO. __510__

Date	Explanation	Post Ref.	Debit	Credit	Balance Debit	Balance Credit

PURCHASES RETURNS AND ALLOWANCES   ACCOUNT NO. __512__

Date	Explanation	Post Ref.	Debit	Credit	Balance Debit	Balance Credit

PROBLEM 10A-4 OR PROBLEM 10B-4 (CONCLUDED)

PURCHASES DISCOUNT   **ACCOUNT NO. 514**

Date	Explanation	Post Ref.	Debit	Credit	Balance Debit	Balance Credit

SALARIES EXPENSE   **ACCOUNT NO. 610**

Date	Explanation	Post Ref.	Debit	Credit	Balance Debit	Balance Credit

CLEANING EXPENSE   **ACCOUNT NO. 612**

Date	Explanation	Post Ref.	Debit	Credit	Balance Debit	Balance Credit

CHAPTER 10
SUMMARY PRACTICE TEST
SPECIAL JOURNALS:
PURCHASES AND CASH PAYMENTS

Part I Instructions

Fill in the blank(s) to complete the statement.

1. F.O.B. shipping point means the _____ covers the shipping cost.
2. Purchases are categorized as _____.
3. The Purchases account has a _____ balance.
4. Purchases are defined as merchandise for _____ to customers.
5. The accounts payable subsidiary ledger represents a potential _____ of cash.
6. The controlling account in the general ledger for the accounts payable subsidiary ledger is called _____ _____.
7. The accounts payable subsidiary ledger would be recorded _____.
8. The balance in the Accounts Payable controlling account should be equal to the sum of the accounts payable ledger accounts _____ _____ _____ _____.
9. The total of the sundry column is _____ _____.
10. The √ in the reference column indicates that the _____ _____ _____ _____ has been updated.
11. A _____ _____ that is issued means the buyer owes less money, as merchandise is being returned or an allowance received.
12. A debit memorandum issued or a credit memorandum received results in a _____ to Accounts Payable and a credit to Purchases, Returns and Allowances.
13. List price - net price = _____ _____ amount.
14. The accounts payable ledger is listed in _____ _____.
15. Purchases Returns and Allowances is increased by a _____.
16. The cash payments journal records transactions that involve outward flows of _____.
17. The cash payments journal alleviates certain repetitive _____.
18. Purchases Discounts is increased by _____.
19. A _____ _____ provides the purchasing department the information to then prepare a purchase order.

20. A _____ _____ is made out after a company inspects received shipments.

21. The total of the cash column is posted at the _____ _____ _____ _____ to the general ledger.

Part II Instructions

From the following chart, complete the statements below.

CASH PAYMENTS JOURNAL

Sundry Dr.			Accounts Payable Dr.		Purchases Discounts Cr.		Cash Cr.	
			X X X		X X X		X X X	(E)
			X X X	(G)	X X X	(F)	X X X	
			X X X	(J)			X X X	
X X X	(H)						X X X	
X X X	(I)						X X X	
X X X			X X X		X X X		X X X	
(A)			(B)		(C)		(D)	

1. EXAMPLE: A is *never posted.*

2. B is posted at _____ _____ _____ in the general ledger to Accounts Payable.

3. C is posted monthly to _____ _____ in the _____ _____ at the end of the month.

4. D is posted as a _____ balance at the end of the month to Cash in the general ledger.

5. E is _____ _____, because the total of cash is posted at the end of the month.

6. F need not be _____, as the column total is posted at the end of the month to the general ledger.

7. G is _____ _____ to the accounts payable ledger.

8. H is posted during the month to the _____ _____.

9. I is _____ _____ the month to the general ledger.

10. J is recorded _____ to the accounts payable subsidiary ledger.

Part III Instructions

Answer true or false to the following statements.

1. F.O.B shipping point means buyer is responsible to cover shipping costs.
2. The purchases account is a contra-cost of goods sold account.
3. Purchases Discounts are the result of paying for equipment within the discount period.
4. F.O.B. Destination means the seller is responsible to cover shipping costs.
5. Purchases Discounts are taken on freight.
6. The purchases journal records only the buying of merchandise.
7. The cash payments journal records the receipt of cash.
8. The balance in Accounts Payable, the controlling account, will be equal to the sum of the accounts receivable subsidiary ledger at the end of the month.
9. A purchase order is completed after the purchase requisition.
10. On receiving a purchase order, the seller may issue a sales invoice.
11. The normal balance of Purchases Discount is a debit balance.
12. The seller wil often issue a debit memorandum to the buyer.
13. All credit memorandums must be recorded in general journals.
14. Returned equipment by a buyer results in a change in Purchases Returns and Allowances.
15. Trade discounts do not occur because of early payments of one's bills.
16. A seller's sales discount on purchases is the buyers purchases discount.
17. Buying of equipment on account is only recorded in the general ledger.
18. On receiving a debit memorandum, the seller will issue a credit memorandum.
19. Cash sales are recorded in the cash payments journal.
20. Purchases are contra costs.

CHAPTER 10
SOLUTIONS TO SUMMARY PRACTICE TEST

Part I

1. buyer (purchaser)
2. cost
3. debit
4. resale
5. outflow
6. accounts payable
7. daily
8. at end of month
9. never posted
10. accounts payable subsidiary ledger
11. debit memorandum
12. debit
13. trade discount
14. alphabetical order
15. credit
16. cash
17. postings
18. credits
19. purchase requisition
20. receiving report
21. end of the month

Part II

1. never posted
2. end of month
3. Purchases Discounts, general ledger
4. credit
5. not posted

6. posted
7. recorded immediatly (or daily)
8. general ledger
9. posted during
10. daily

Part III

1. true
2. false
3. false
4. true
5. false
6. false
7. false
8. false
9. true
10. true

11. false
12. false
13. false
14. false
15. true
16. true
17. false
18. true
19. false
20. false

CHAPTERS 1-10
ACCOUNTING RECALL FORMS

Part I

1. _____

2. _____

3. _____

4. _____

5. _____

6. _____

7. _____

8. _____

9. _____

10. _____

Part II

11. _____

12. _____

13. _____

14. _____

15. _____

CONTINUING PROBLEM FOR CHAPTER 10

PURCHASES JOURNAL

PAGE 1

Date	Account Credited	PR	Accounts Payable Cr.	Purchases Dr.	Sundry Dr.		
					Account	PR	Amount

CASH PAYMENT JOURNAL

PAGE 1

Date	Check No.	Accounts Debited	PR.	Sundry Account Dr.	Accounts Payable Dr.	Purchases Discounts Cr.	Cash Cr.

ELDORADO COMPUTER CENTER
GENERAL JOURNAL

PAGE 11

Date	Account Titles and Description	PR	Dr.	Cr.

PARTIAL GENERAL LEDGER

CASH   ACCOUNT NO. 1000

Date		Explanation	Post Ref.	Debit	Credit	Balance	
						Debit	Credit
2/1	XX	Balance forward	√			15 1 1 6 65	

SUPPLIES   ACCOUNT NO. 1030

Date		Explanation	Post Ref.	Debit	Credit	Balance	
						Debit	Credit
2/1	XX	Balance forward	√			1 3 2 00	

MERCHANDISE INVENTORY   ACCOUNT NO. 1040

Date	Explanation	Post Ref.	Debit	Credit	Balance	
					Debit	Credit

PREPAID RENT   ACCOUNT NO. 1025

Date		Explanation	Post Ref.	Debit	Credit	Balance Debit	Balance Credit
2/1	XX	Balance forward	√			1 6 0 0 00	

ACCOUNTS PAYABLE   ACCOUNT NO. 2000

Date		Explanation	Post Ref.	Debit	Credit	Balance Debit	Balance Credit
2/1	XX	Balance forward	√				2 0 5 0 00

PURCHASES   ACCOUNT NO. 6000

Date	Explanation	Post Ref.	Debit	Credit	Balance Debit	Balance Credit

PURCHASE RETURNS AND ALLOWANCES   ACCOUNT NO. 6010

Date	Explanation	Post Ref.	Debit	Credit	Balance Debit	Balance Credit

PURCHASE DISOUNTS   ACCOUNT NO. 6020

Date	Explanation	Post Ref.	Debit	Credit	Balance Debit	Balance Credit

ELDORADO COMPUTER CENTER
SCHEDULE OF ACCOUNTS PAYABLE
2/28/XX

ACCOUNTS PAYABLE SUBSIDIARY LEDGER

NAME   MULTI SYSTEMS   # 6A3

ADDRESS   1919 MORAN ST., ANAHEIM, CA 92606

Date		Explanation	Post Ref.	Debit	Credit	Cr. Balance
2/1	XX	Balance forward	√			4 5 0 00

NAME   OFFICE DEPOT   # 6A4

ADDRESS   460 ESCONDIDO BLVD., ESCONDIDO, CA 92025

Date		Explanation	Post Ref.	Debit	Credit	Cr. Balance
2/1	XX	Balance forward	√			5 0 00

NAME   SAN DIEGO ELECTRIC   # 6A5

ADDRESS   606 INDUSTRIAL ST., SAN DIEGO, CA 92121

Date		Explanation	Post Ref.	Debit	Credit	Cr. Balance

NAME   PACIFIC BELL   # 6A6

ADDRESS   101 BELL AVE., SAN DIEGO, CA 92101

Date		Explanation	Post Ref.	Debit	Credit	Cr. Balance
2/1	XX	Balance forward	√			1 5 0 00

NAME   COMPUTER CONNECTION   # 6A7

ADDRESS   1020 WIL LANE, LOS ANGELES, CA 92405

Date		Explanation	Post Ref.	Debit	Credit	Cr. Balance

NAME	SYSTEMS DESIGN FURNITURE		# 6A8
ADDRESS	2070 FIRST ST., SAN DIEGO, CA 92101		

Date		Explanation	Post Ref.	Debit	Credit	Cr. Balance
2/1	XX	Balance forward	√			1 4 0 0 00

SOLUTIONS TO ACCOUNTING RECALL

Part I

1.	J	**6.**	I
2.	E	**7.**	F
3.	C	**8.**	B
4.	D	**9.**	H
5.	A	**10.**	G

Part II

11. False; Sales Returns and Allowances

12. False; Credit

13. True

14. False; Credit

15. True

Appendix A
Working Papers for
Simply Accounting
Computer Workshops

Materials Prepared By

Sylvia Hearing
Clackamas Community College

COMPUTER WORKSHOP (CHAPTER 3)
Journalizing, Posting, General Ledger, Trial Balance, and Chart of Accounts

REPORT TRANSMITTAL   Student Name_____

The Atlas Company

A. Attach the following reports:

1. General Journal 12/1/97 to 12/31/97.

2. General Ledger Report 12/1/97 to 12/31/97.

3. Trial Balance As At 12/31/97.

4. Chart of Accounts As At 12/31/97.

B. Refer to your reports to list the amounts requested below:

1. Cash account balance $_____

2. Accounts Receivable account balance $_____

3. Accounts Payable account balance $_____

4. Owner's, Withdrawals account balance $_____

5. Fees Earned account balance $_____

COMPUTER WORKSHOP (CHAPTER 4)
Compound Journal Entries, Adjusting Entries, and Financial Reports

REPORT TRANSMITTAL   Student Name_____
The Zell Company

A. Attach the following reports:

1. General Journal 12/1/97 to 12/31/97.

2. Trial Balance As At 12/31/97.

3. General Journal 12/31/97 to 12/31/97.

4. General Ledger Report 12/1/97 to 12/31/97.

5. Trial Balance As At 12/31/97 (after the adjusting entries have been recorded).

6. Income Statement 1/1/97 to 12/31/97.

7. Balance Sheet As At 12/31/97.

B. Refer to your reports to list the amounts requested below:

1. Net Income $_____

2. Total Assets $_____

3. Total Operating Expenses $_____

4. Owner's, Withdrawals account balance $_____

5. Total Liabilities $_____

COMPUTER WORKSHOP
(VALDEZ REALTY MINI PRACTICE SET)
Closing Process and Post-Closing Trial Balance

REPORT TRANSMITTAL FOR JUNE   Student Name_____
Valdez Realty

A. Attach the following reports:

1. General Journal 6/1/97 to 6/30/97.

2. Trial Balance As At 6/30/97.

3. General Journal 6/1/97 to 6/30/97 (after the adjusting entries have been recorded).

4. Trial Balance As At 6/30/97 (after the adjusting entries have been recorded).

5. General Ledger Report 6/1/97 to 6/30/97.

6. Income Statement 6/1/97 to 6/30/97.

7. Balance Sheet As At 6/30/97.

8. Trial Balance As At 7/1/97.

B. Refer to your reports to list the amounts requested below:

1. Net Income $_____

2. Total Assets $_____

3. Total Operating Expenses $_____

4. Total Liabilities $_____

5. Owner's, Capital account balance on the 7/1/97 Trial Balance $_____

COMPUTER WORKSHOP
(VALDEZ REALTY MINI PRACTICE SET)
Closing Process and Post-Closing Trial Balance

REPORT TRANSMITTAL FOR JULY   Student Name_____

Valdez Realty

A. Attach the following reports:

1. General Journal 7/1/97 to 7/31/97.

2. Trial Balance As At 7/31/97.

3. General Journal 7/1/97 to 7/31/97 (after the adjusting entries have been recorded).

4. Trial Balance As At 7/31/97 (after the adjusting entries have been recorded).

5. General Ledger Report 7/1/97 to 7/31/97.

6. Income Statement 7/1/97 to 7/31/97.

7. Balance Sheet As At 7/31/97.

8. Trial Balance As At 8/1/97.

B. Refer to your reports to list the amounts requested below:

1. Net Income $_____

2. Total Assets $_____

3. Total Operating Expenses $_____

4. Total Liabilities $_____

5. Owner's, Capital account balance on the 8/1/97 Trial Balance $_____

COMPUTER WORKSHOP
(PETE'S MARKET MINI PRACTICE SET)
Completing Payroll Requirements for First Quarter and Preparing Form 941

REPORT TRANSMITTAL   Student Name_____
Pete's Market

A. Attach the following reports:

1.   Employee Detail 1/1/97 to 1/31/97.
2.   General Journal 1/1/97 to 1/31/97.
3.   Trial Balance As At 1/31/97.
4.   Employee Detail 2/1/97 to 2/28/97.
5.   General Journal 2/1/97 to 2/28/97.
6.   Trial Balance As At 2/28/97.
7.   Employee Detail 3/1/97 to 3/31/97.
8.   General Journal 3/1/97 to 3/31/97.
9.   Trial Balance As At 3/31/97.
10. 941 FIT Summary 3/31/97.
11. 941 Social Security/Medicare Summary 3/31/97.
12. General Journal 4/1/97 to 4/30/97.
13. Trial Balance As At 4/30/97.

B. Refer to your reports to list the amounts requested below:

1. Cash account balance on 4/30/97 Trial Balance $_____

2. Payroll Checking Cash account balance on 4/30/97 Trial Balance $_____

3. Wages account balance on 1/31/97 Trial Balance $_____

4. Social Security Tax Expense account balance on 2/28/97 Trial Balance $_____

5. SUTA Expense account balance on 3/31/97 Trial Balance $_____

C. Prepare Form 941 for the first quarter.

Form **941**
(Rev. April 1994)
Department of the Treasury
Internal Revenue Service

4141

Employer's Quarterly Federal Tax Return

▶ See separate instructions for information on completing this return.

Please type or print.

OMB No. 1545-0029

Enter state code for state in which deposits made . ▶ ☐
(see page 2 of instructions).

Name (as distinguished from trade name)	Date quarter ended
Trade name, if any	Employer identification number
Address (number and street)	City, state, and ZIP code

T	
FF	
FD	
FP	
I	
T	

If address is different from prior return, check here ▶ ☐

IRS Use

```
1 1 1 1 1 1 1 1 1 1    2    3 3 3 3 3 3    4 4 4
5 5 5   6   7   8 8 8 8 8 8   9 9 9   10 10 10 10 10 10 10 10 10 10
```

If you do not have to file returns in the future, check here ▶ ☐ and enter date final wages paid ▶ _____

If you are a seasonal employer, see **Seasonal employers** on page 2 and check here (see instructions) ▶ ☐

1	Number of employees (except household) employed in the pay period that includes March 12th ▶		
2	Total wages and tips subject to withholding, plus other compensation	**2**	
3	Total income tax withheld from wages, tips, and sick pay	**3**	
4	Adjustment of withheld income tax for preceding quarters of calendar year	**4**	
5	Adjusted total of income tax withheld (line 3 as adjusted by line 4—see instructions) . . .	**5**	
6a	Taxable social security wages . . . . . . $ _____ × 12.4% (.124) =	**6a**	
b	Taxable social security tips . . . . $ _____ × 12.4% (.124) =	**6b**	
7	Taxable Medicare wages and tips . . . . . $ _____ × 2.9% (.029) =	**7**	
8	Total social security and Medicare taxes (add lines 6a, 6b, and 7). Check here if wages are not subject to social security and/or Medicare tax . . . . ▶ ☐	**8**	
9	Adjustment of social security and Medicare taxes (see instructions for required explanation) Sick Pay $ _____ ± Fractions of Cents $ _____ ± Other $ _____ =	**9**	
10	Adjusted total of social security and Medicare taxes (line 8 as adjusted by line 9—see instructions)	**10**	
11	**Total taxes** (add lines 5 and 10)	**11**	
12	Advance earned income credit (EIC) payments made to employees, if any	**12**	
13	Net taxes (subtract line 12 from line 11). **This should equal line 17, column (d) below** (or line D of Schedule B (Form 941))	**13**	
14	Total deposits for quarter, including overpayment applied from a prior quarter	**14**	
15	**Balance due** (subtract line 14 from line 13). Pay to Internal Revenue Service	**15**	
16	**Overpayment,** if line 14 is more than line 13, enter excess here ▶ $ _____ and check if to be: ☐ Applied to next return **OR** ☐ Refunded.		

• **All filers:** If line 13 is less than $500, you need not complete line 17 or Schedule B.

• **Semiweekly depositors:** Complete Schedule B and check here . . . . ▶ ☐

• **Monthly depositors:** Complete line 17, columns (a) through (d) and check here . . . . . . ▶ ☐

17	**Monthly Summary of Federal Tax Liability.**			
	(a) First month liability	**(b)** Second month liability	**(c)** Third month liability	**(d)** Total liability for quarter

Sign Here

Under penalties of perjury, I declare that I have examined this return, including accompanying schedules and statements, and to the best of my knowledge and belief, it is true, correct, and complete.

Signature ▶ _____   Print Your Name and Title ▶ _____   Date ▶ _____

For Paperwork Reduction Act Notice, see page 1 of separate instructions.   Cat. No. 17001Z   Form **941** (Rev. 4-94)

*U.S. Government Printing Office: 1994 — 301-628/00153

COMPUTER WORKSHOP (CHAPTER 10)
Part A: Recording Transactions in the Sales, Receipts, Purchases, and Payments Journals

REPORT TRANSMITTAL   Student Name_____
The Mars Company

A. Attach the following reports:

1. Customer Aged Detail As at 3/31/97.

2. Vendor Aged Detail As at 3/31/97.

3. General Journal 3/1/97 to 3/31/97.

4. General Ledger Report 3/1/97 to 3/31/97.

B. Refer to your reports to list the amounts requested below:

1. Customer Aged Detail report total $_____

2. Vendor Aged Detail report total $_____

3. Amount owed by customer Kevin Tucker $_____

4. Amount owed to vendor Pat Young $_____

5. Cash account balance $_____

COMPUTER WORKSHOP (CHAPTER 10)
Part B: Computerized Accounting Instructions for Abby's Toy House (Problem 10 A-4)

REPORT TRANSMITTAL   Student Name_____
Abby's Toy House

A. Attach the following reports:

1. Customer Aged Detail As at 3/31/97.

2. Vendor Aged Detail As at 3/31/97.

3. General Journal 3/1/97 to 3/31/97.

4. General Ledger Report 3/1/97 to 3/31/97.

B. Refer to your reports to list the amounts requested below:

1. Customer Aged Detail report total $_____

2. Vendor Aged Detail report total $_____

3. Amount owed by customer Bill Burton $_____

4. Amount owed to vendor Earl Miller Company $_____

5. Amount owed to vendor Sam Katz Garage $_____

COMPUTER WORKSHOP
(THE CORNER DRESS SHOP MINI PRACTICE SET)
Inventory Adjusting Entries

REPORT TRANSMITTAL   Student Name_____
The Corner Dress Shop

A. Attach the following reports:

1.   General Journal 3/1/97 to 3/31/97.
2.   Trial Balance As at 3/31/97.
3.   Customer Aged Detail As at 3/31/97.
4.   Vendor Aged Detail As at 3/31/97.
5.   Employee Detail 3/1/97 to 3/31/97.
6.   941 FIT Summary 3/31/97.
7.   941 Social Security/Medicare Summary 3/31/97.
8.   General Journal 3/1/97 to 3/31/97 (after the adjusting entries have been recorded).
9.   Trial Balance As at 3/31/97 (after the adjusting entries have been recorded).
10. General Ledger Report 3/1/97 to 3/31/97.
11. Income Statement 3/1/97 to 3/31/97.
12. Balance Sheet As at 3/31/97.
13. Trial Balance As at 4/1/97.

B. Refer to your reports to list the amounts requested below:

1. Net Income $_____

2. Total Assets $_____

3. Total Operating Expenses $_____

4. Total Cost of Goods Sold $_____

5. Betty Loeb's, Capital account balance on the 4/1/97 Trial Balance $_____

C. Complete Form 941 and sign it as of the last day in April. Assume that the FIT, Social Security, and Medicare taxes for the March payroll were paid in full on 4/15/97. Additional information for use in completing Form 941:

    Monthly Summary of Federal Tax Liability.
    (a) First month liability $2,565.21

Employer's Quarterly Federal Tax Return

▶ See separate instructions for information on completing this return.

Please type or print.

OMB No. 1545-0029

Enter state
code for
state in
which
deposits
made . ▶
(see
page 2 of
instructions).

Name (as distinguished from trade name)

Date quarter ended

Trade name, if any

Employer identification number

Address (number and street)

City, state, and ZIP code

| T |
| FF |
| FD |
| FP |
| I |
| T |

If address is
different
from prior
return, check
here ▶

IRS Use

1	1	1	1	1	1	1	1	1	1	2	3	3	3	3	3	4	4	4							
5	5	5	6		7		8	8	8	8	8	9	9	9		10	10	10	10	10	10	10	10	10	10

If you do not have to file returns in the future, check here ▶ ☐ and enter date final wages paid ▶

If you are a seasonal employer, see **Seasonal employers** on page 2 and check here (see instructions) ▶ ☐

1	Number of employees (except household) employed in the pay period that includes March 12th ▶		
2	Total wages and tips subject to withholding, plus other compensation	**2**	
3	Total income tax withheld from wages, tips, and sick pay	**3**	
4	Adjustment of withheld income tax for preceding quarters of calendar year . .	**4**	
5	Adjusted total of income tax withheld (line 3 as adjusted by line 4—see instructions)	**5**	
6a	Taxable social security wages . . . . $ _____ × 12.4% (.124) =	**6a**	
b	Taxable social security tips . . . . $ _____ × 12.4% (.124) =	**6b**	
7	Taxable Medicare wages and tips . . . . . $ _____ × 2.9% (.029) =	**7**	
8	Total social security and Medicare taxes (add lines 6a, 6b, and 7). Check here if wages are not subject to social security and/or Medicare tax . . . . ▶ ☐	**8**	
9	Adjustment of social security and Medicare taxes (see instructions for required explanation) Sick Pay $ _____ ± Fractions of Cents $ _____ ± Other $ _____ =	**9**	
10	Adjusted total of social security and Medicare taxes (line 8 as adjusted by line 9—see instructions)	**10**	
11	**Total taxes** (add lines 5 and 10)	**11**	
12	Advance earned income credit (EIC) payments made to employees, if any	**12**	
13	Net taxes (subtract line 12 from line 11). **This should equal line 17, column (d) below** (or line D of Schedule B (Form 941))	**13**	
14	Total deposits for quarter, including overpayment applied from a prior quarter	**14**	
15	**Balance due** (subtract line 14 from line 13). Pay to Internal Revenue Service	**15**	

16 **Overpayment,** if line 14 is more than line 13, enter excess here ▶ $ _____

and check if to be: ☐ Applied to next return **OR** ☐ Refunded.

- **All filers:** If line 13 is less than $500, you need not complete line 17 or Schedule B.
- **Semiweekly depositors:** Complete Schedule B and check here . . . . ▶ ☐
- **Monthly depositors:** Complete line 17, columns (a) through (d) and check here . . . . . ▶ ☐

17	**Monthly Summary of Federal Tax Liability.**			
	(a) First month liability	**(b)** Second month liability	**(c)** Third month liability	**(d)** Total liability for quarter

**Sign
Here**

Under penalties of perjury, I declare that I have examined this return, including accompanying schedules and statements, and to the best of my knowledge and belief, it is true, correct, and complete.

Signature ▶

Print Your
Name and Title ▶

Date ▶

For Paperwork Reduction Act Notice, see page 1 of separate instructions.   Cat. No. 17001Z   Form **941** (Rev. 4-94)

COMPUTER WORKSHOP (CHAPTER 16)
Perpetual Inventory System

REPORT TRANSMITTAL   Student Name_____
The Paint Place

A. Attach the following reports:

1. Inventory Activity Detail Report 3/1/97 to 3/31/97.

2. Inventory Synopsis 3/31/97.

3. General Journal 3/1/97 to 3/31/97.

4. Trial Balance As At 3/31/97.

5. Customer Aged Detail As at 3/31/97.

6. Vendor Aged Detail As at 3/31/97.

7. Income Statement 1/1/97 to 3/31/97.

8. Balance Sheet As At 3/31/97.

B. Refer to your reports to list the amounts requested below:

1. Total value of the Latex Semi-gloss inventory item $_____

2. Total value of the Merchandise Inventory $_____

3. Cost of Goods Sold account balance $_____

4. Total value of the Oil Semi-gloss inventory item $_____

5. Net Income $_____